Love is Hidden in Small Places

Nafisa Sekandari & Malia Sekandari

Avagana Publishing
2014

ISBN: 978-0-9909016-0-0
Book Design by: Nafisa Sekandari
Photos by: Nafisa Sekandari, Rahim Sekandari, Ilyas
Sekandari, Aleah Sekandari, Hasina Mojaddidi, Mujghan
Mojaddidi, and Anita Bates.

I dedicate this book to my beautiful and talented daughter Malia Sekandari.

~Acknowledgements~

This book would not be possible without Malia Sekandari's brilliant idea. Her vivid imagination spawned the concept for this book. I am blessed to have such an amazing and creative daughter.

The book would also not be possible without the brilliant eye of Rahim Sekandari, who noticed hearts everywhere he went. Thankfully he captured these moments with his brilliant photographic skills.

Thank you to my wonderful sister, Nelofer Sekandari, for editing.

I'm also grateful to other friends and family for their contribution: Aleah Sekandari, Ilyas Sekandari, Hasina Mojaddidi, Mujghan Mojaddidi, and Brenda Swygert who introduced Anita Bates to me.

When my daughter Malia was 4 years old, she came to me one day with a picture she had drawn and said "look mommy, love is hidden in small places". In her picture she had hidden little hearts for me to find. That inspired us to create a book with pictures of hearts we had found in random places. We wanted the pictures to be authentic and not altered in anyway so for that reason the project has taken us over 5 years to complete. After about 3 years of collecting pictures on our own, we decided to ask other family members for help and luckily several family members responded by sending us pictures they have taken of heart shaped objects they had found. So begins our story of love being hidden in the smallest places. Keep your eyes open to all the beauty around you and you just might see a heart in front of you!

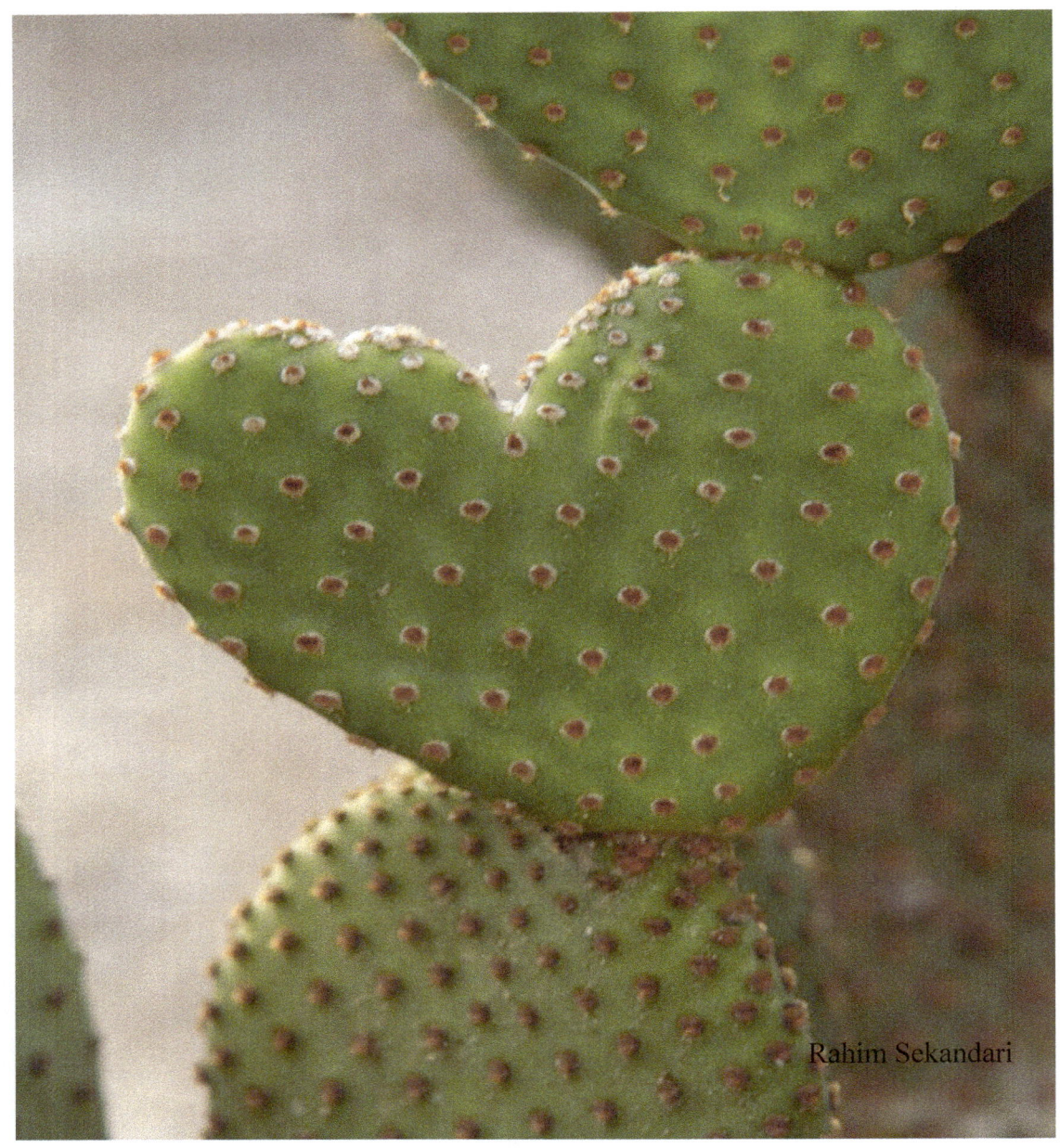

Rahim Sekandari

"Love is a many splendid thing. Love lifts us up where we belong. All you need is love!"
~ Moulin Rouge

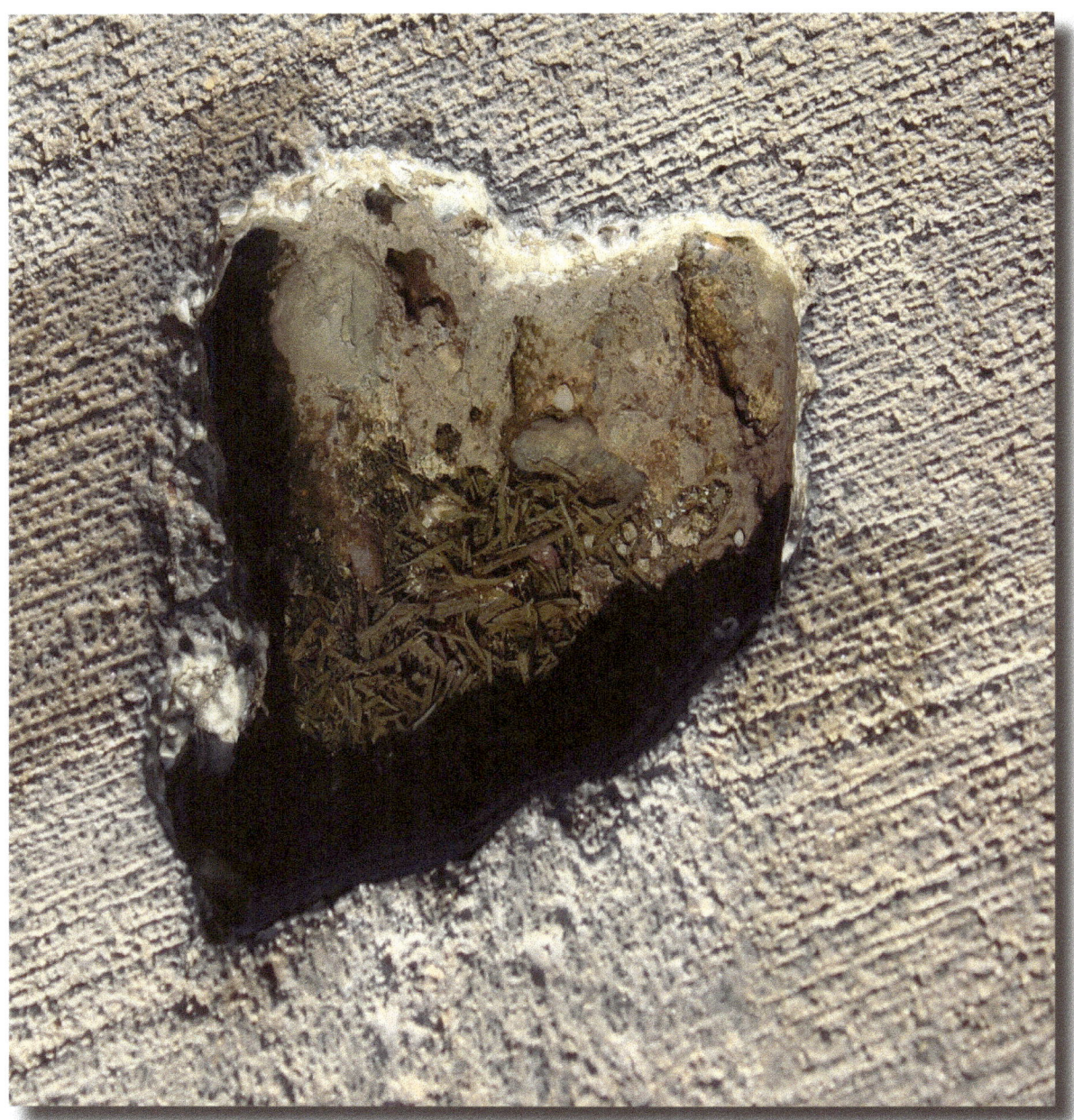

"Love never dies a natural death. It dies because we don't know how to replenish its source. It dies of blindness and errors and betrayals. It dies of illness and wounds; it dies of weariness, of witherings, of tarnishings".

~ Anaïs Nin

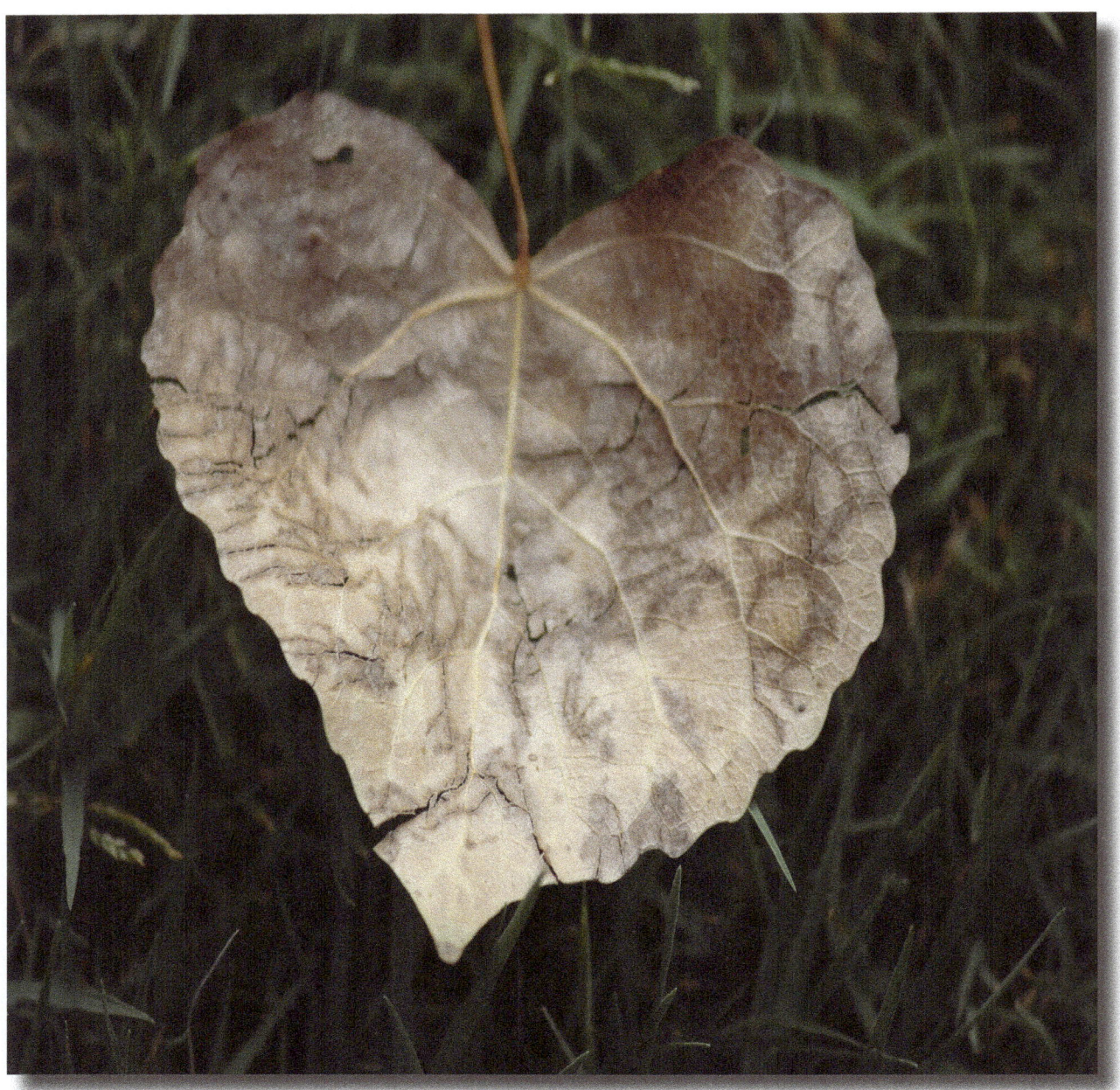

"What lies behind us, and what lies before us are tiny matters compared to what lies within us".

~ Ralph Waldo Emerson

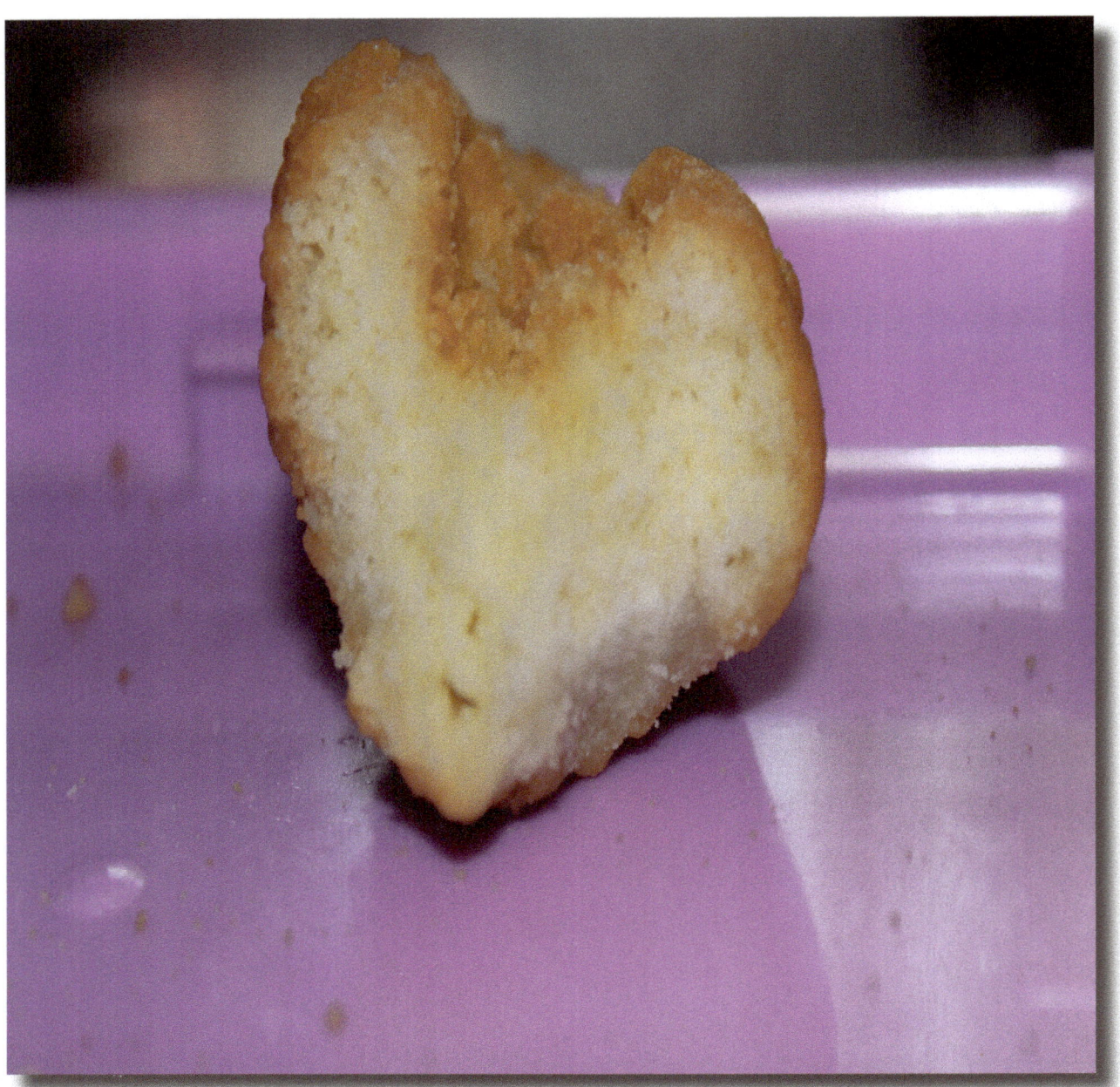

"When you love someone, all your saved up wishes start coming out".

~ Elizabeth Bowen

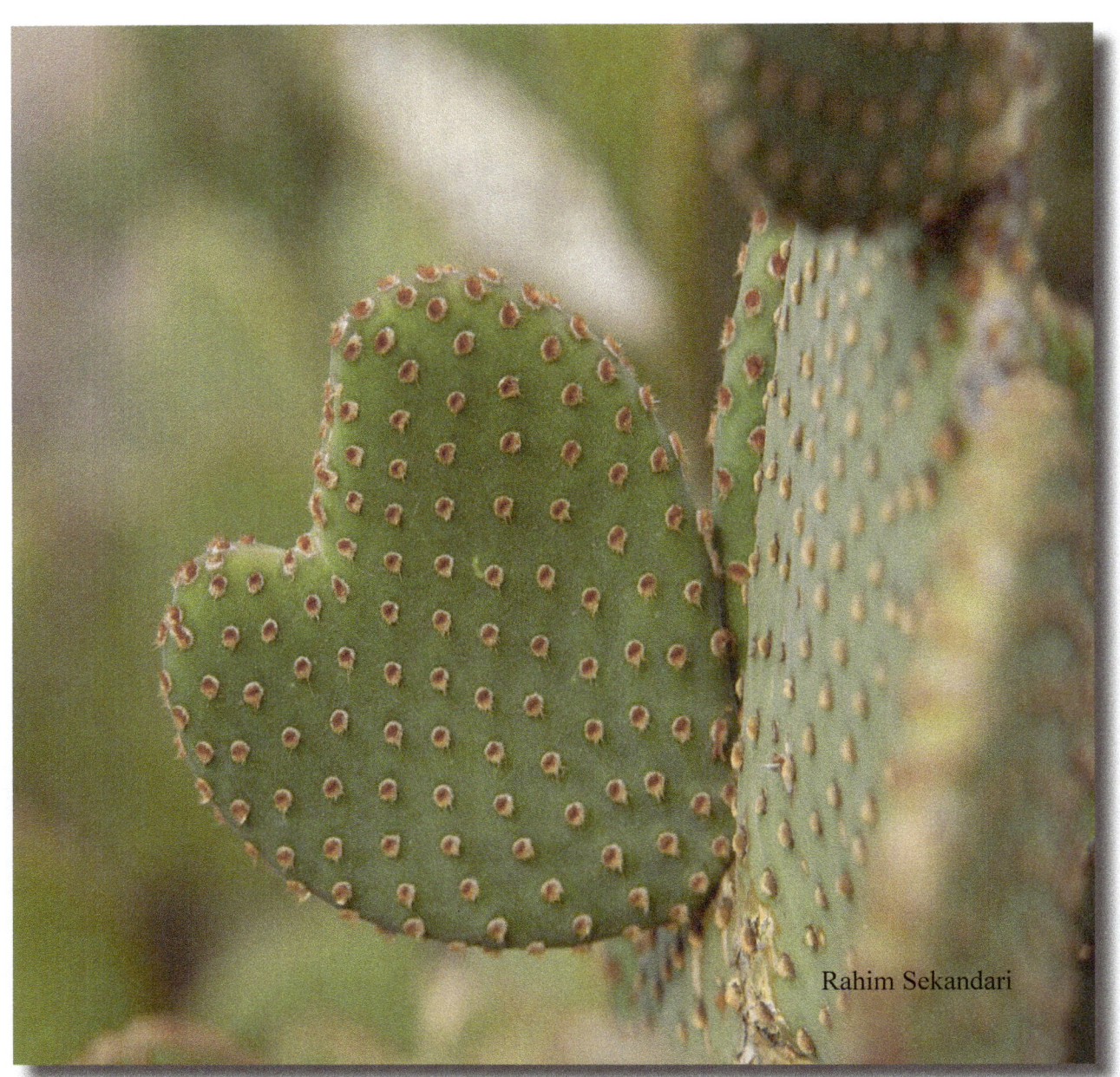

Rahim Sekandari

"I have decided to stick to love; hate is too great a burden to bear."

~Martin Luther King, Jr.

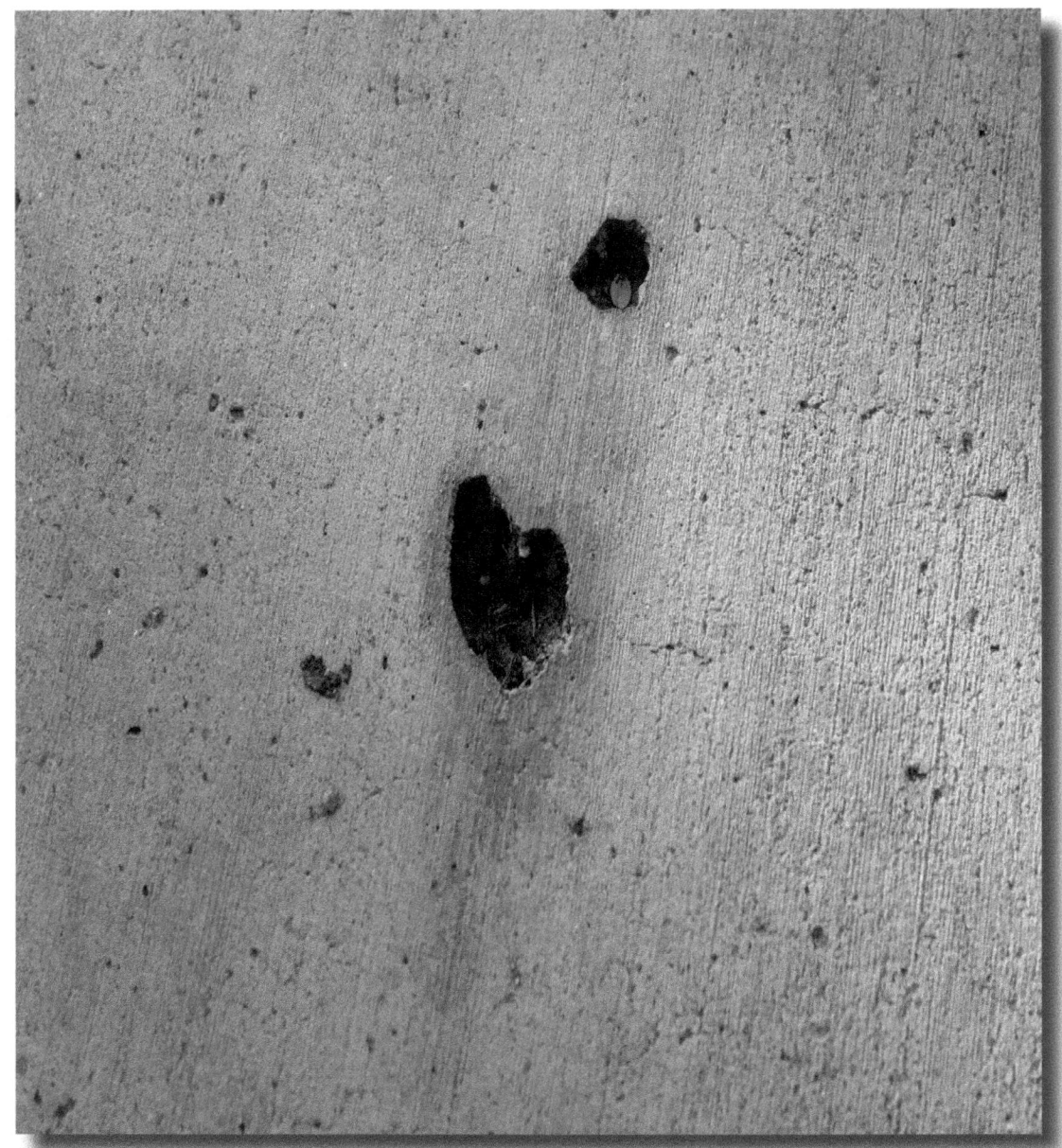

12

"Love is a language spoken by everyone but understood only by the heart".

~Unknown

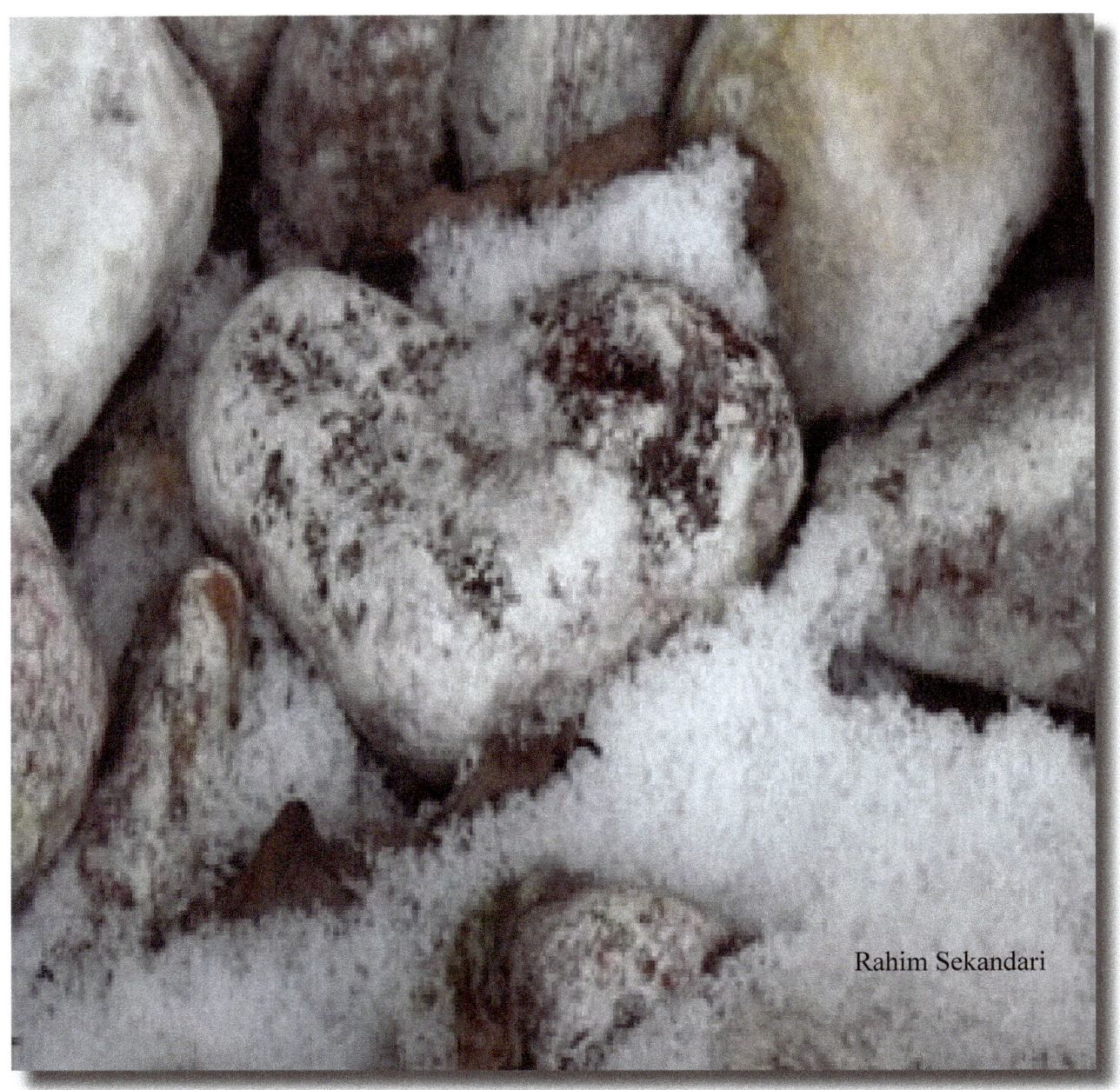

Rahim Sekandari

14

"When you trip over love, it is easy to get up. But when you fall in love, it is impossible to stand again."

~Albert Einstein

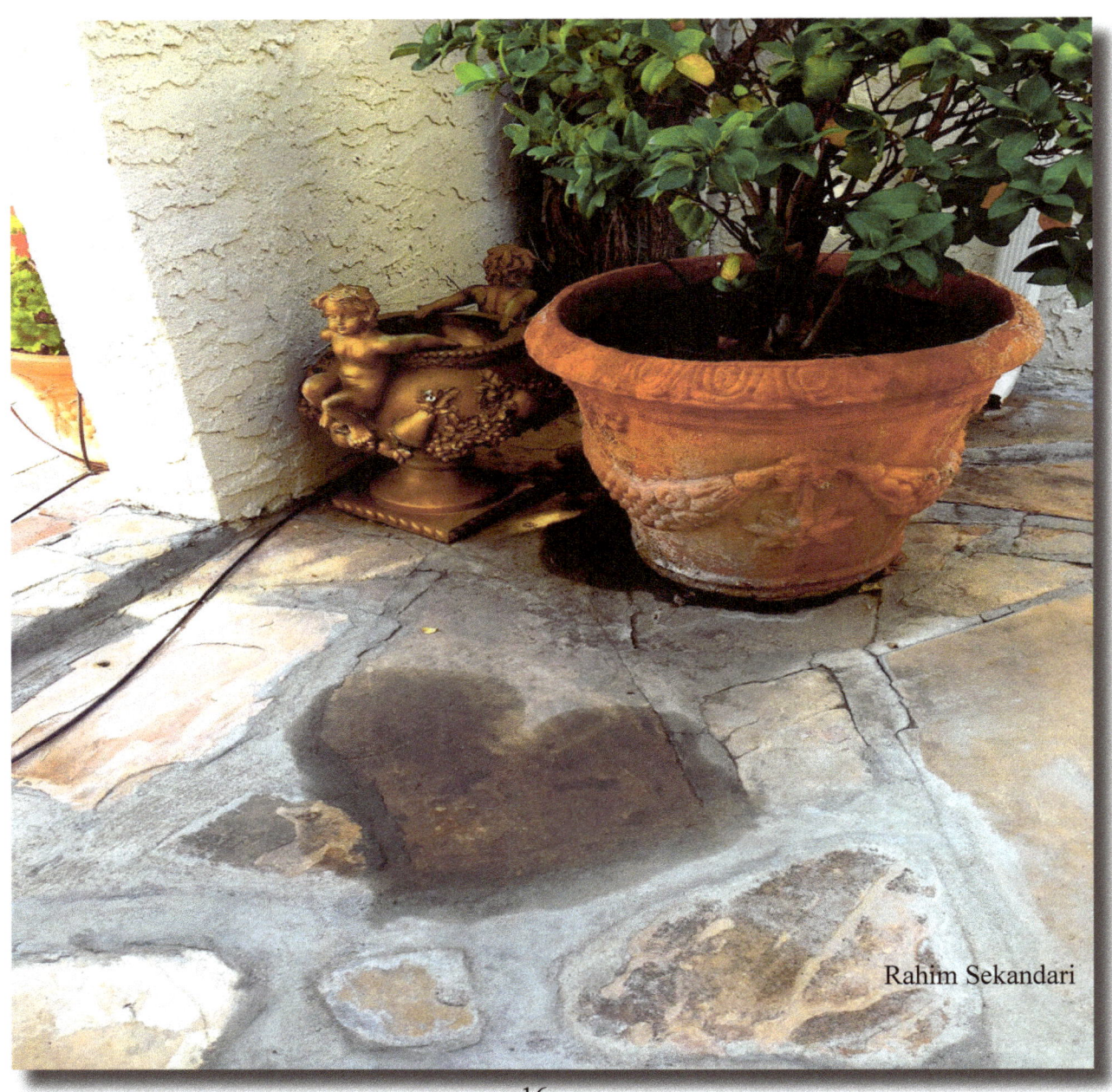

Rahim Sekandari

"Love is a fire. But whether it is going to warm your hearth or burn down your house, you can never tell."

~Joan Crawford

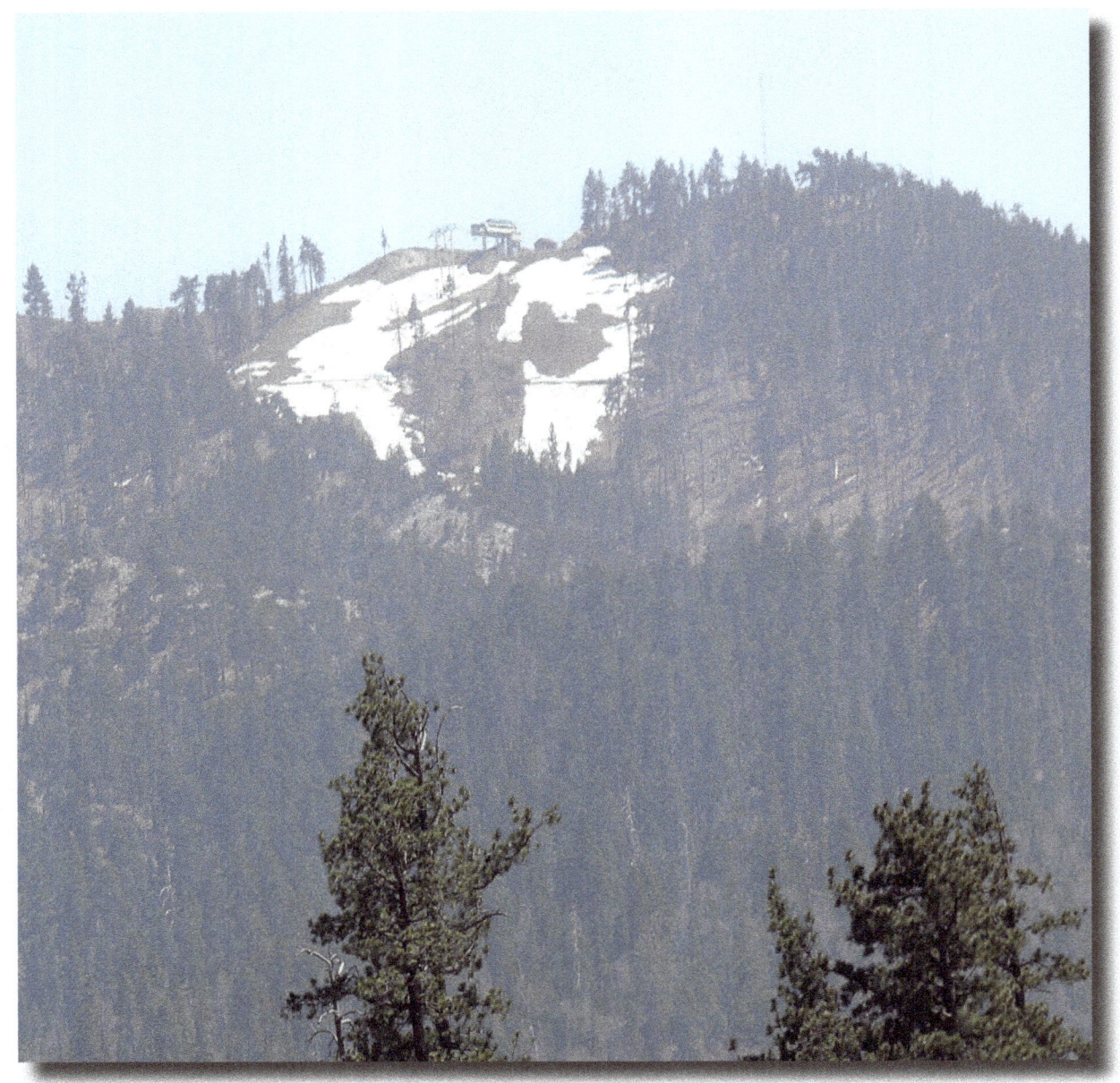

"Love is the voice under all silences, the hope which has no opposite in fear; the strength so strong mere force is feebleness: the truth more first than sun, more last than star"

~ E.E. Cummings

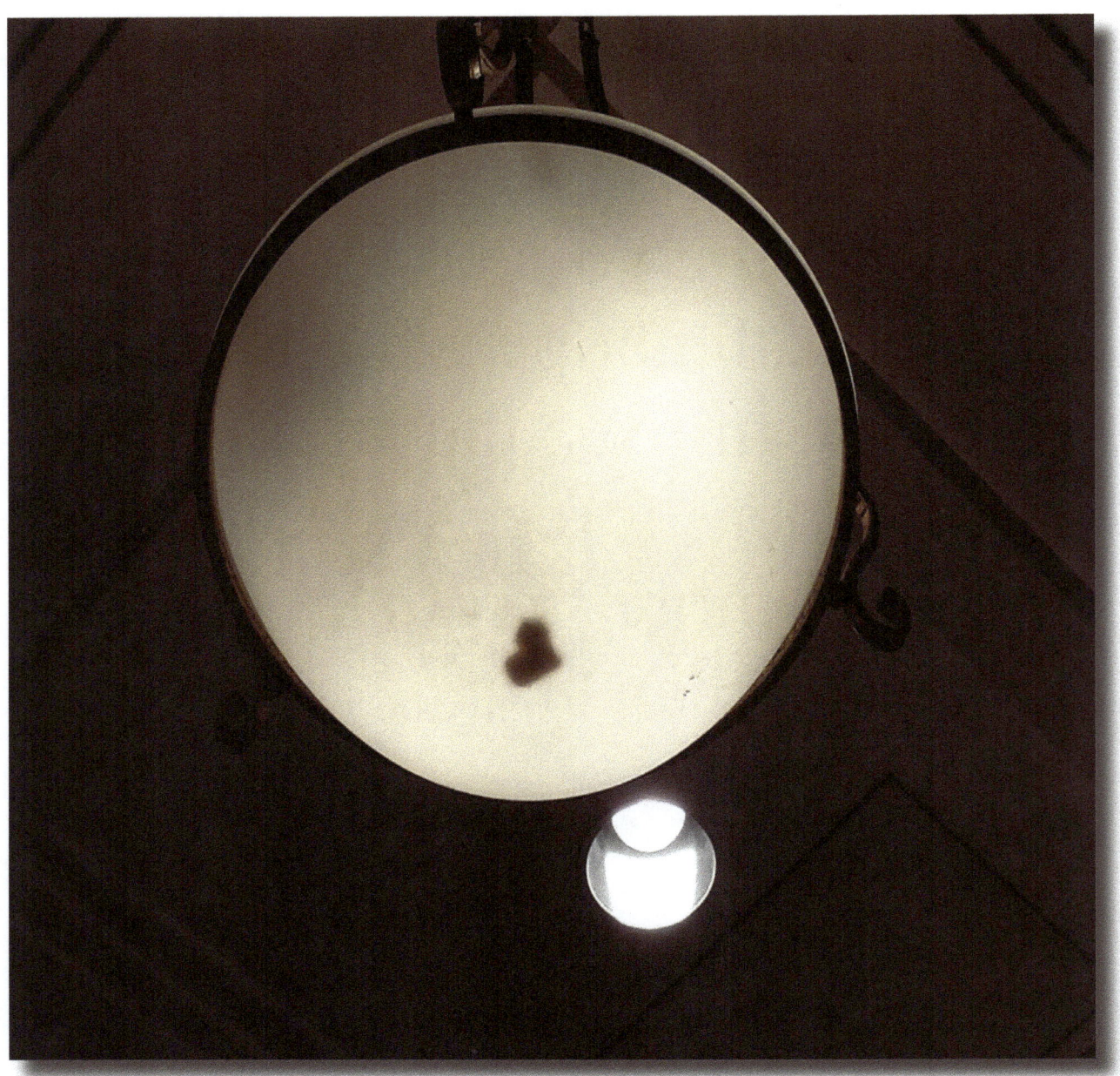

"Love is an untamed force. When we try to control it, it destroys us. When we try to imprison it, it enslaves us. When we try to understand it, it leaves us feeling lost and confused."

~ Paulo Coelho

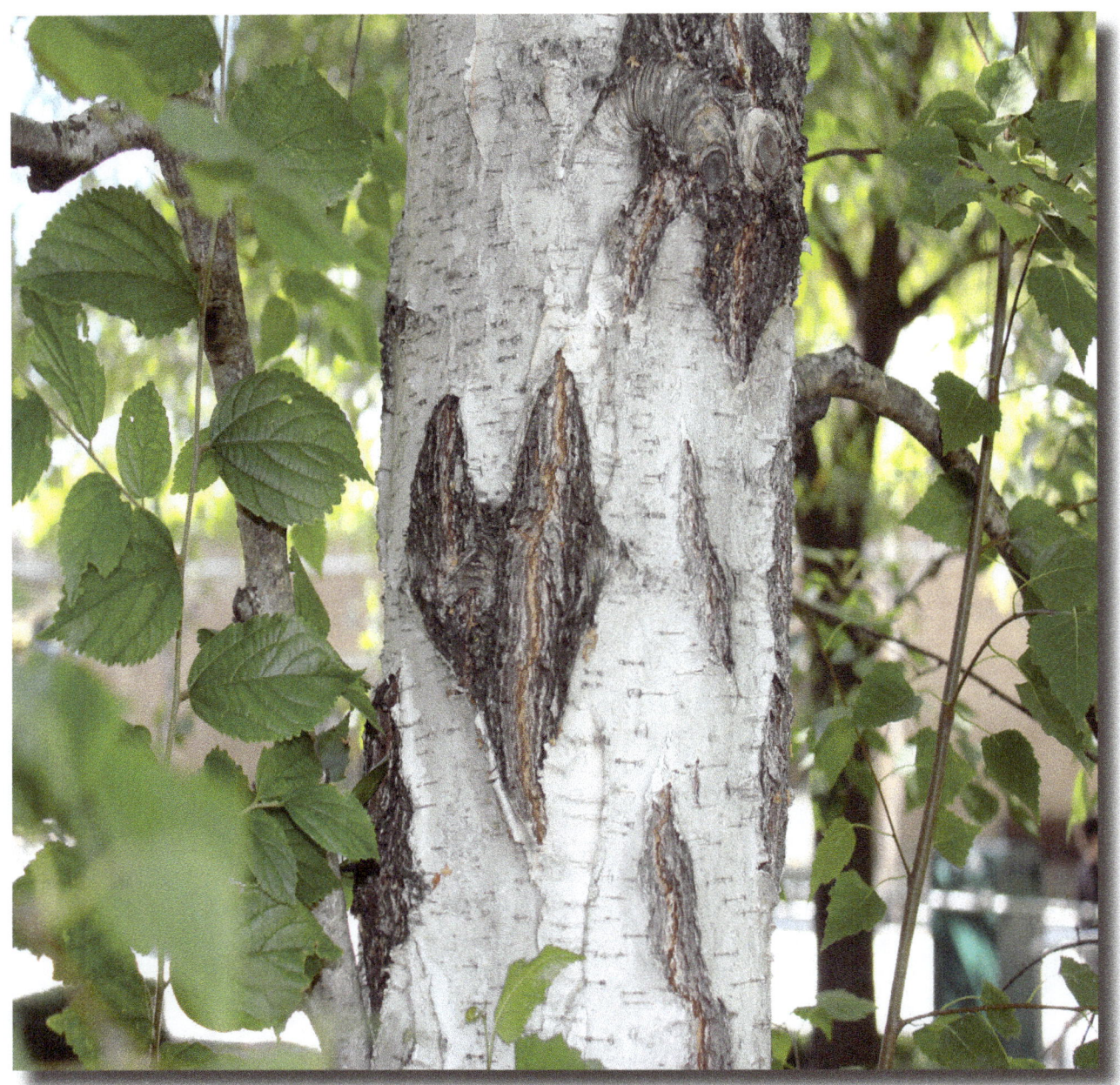

"You know you're in love when you can't fall asleep because reality is finally better than your dreams".

~Dr. Seuss

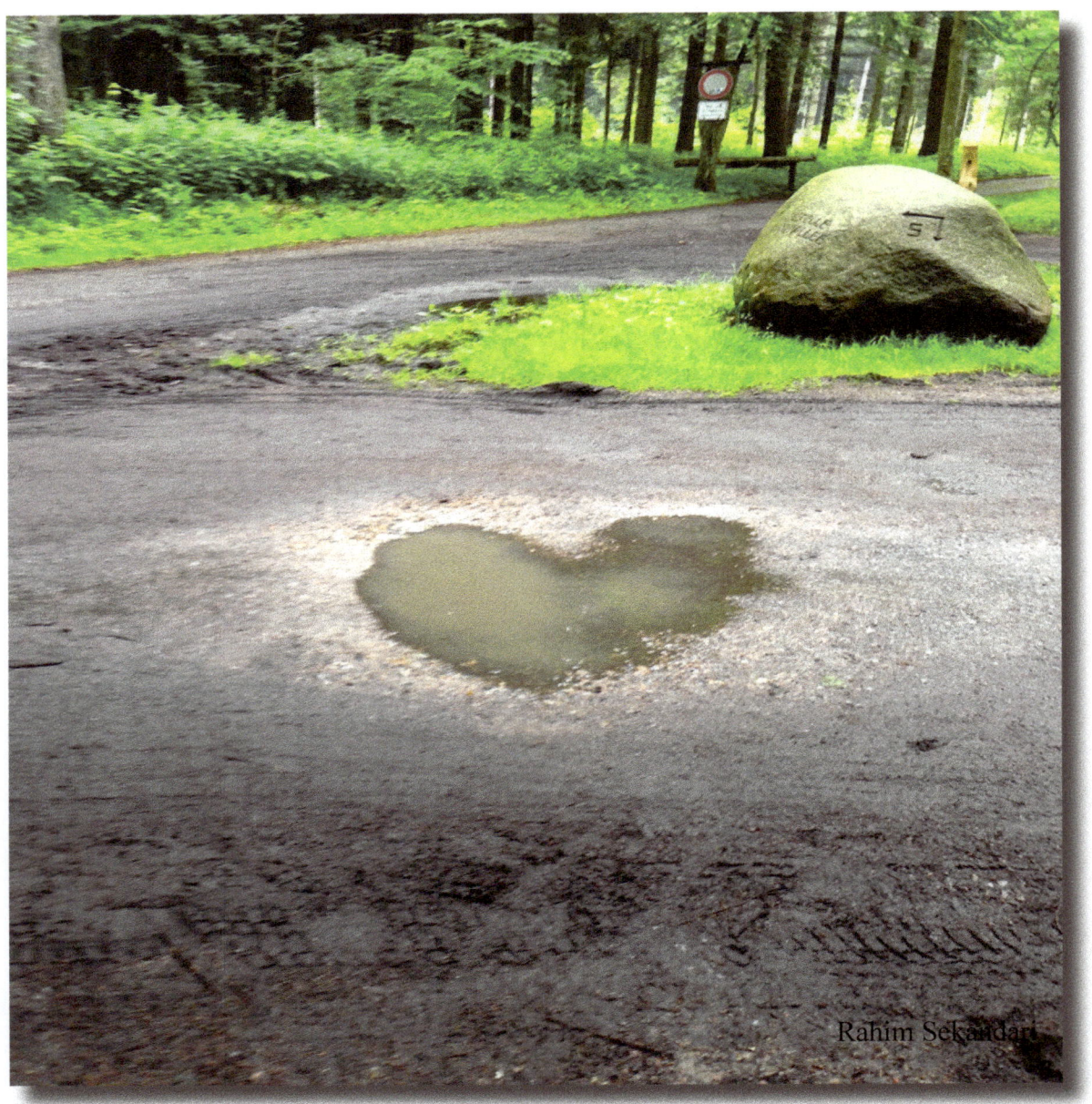

Rahim Sekandari

"Love is like the wind, you can't see it but you can feel it."
~ Nicholas Sparks

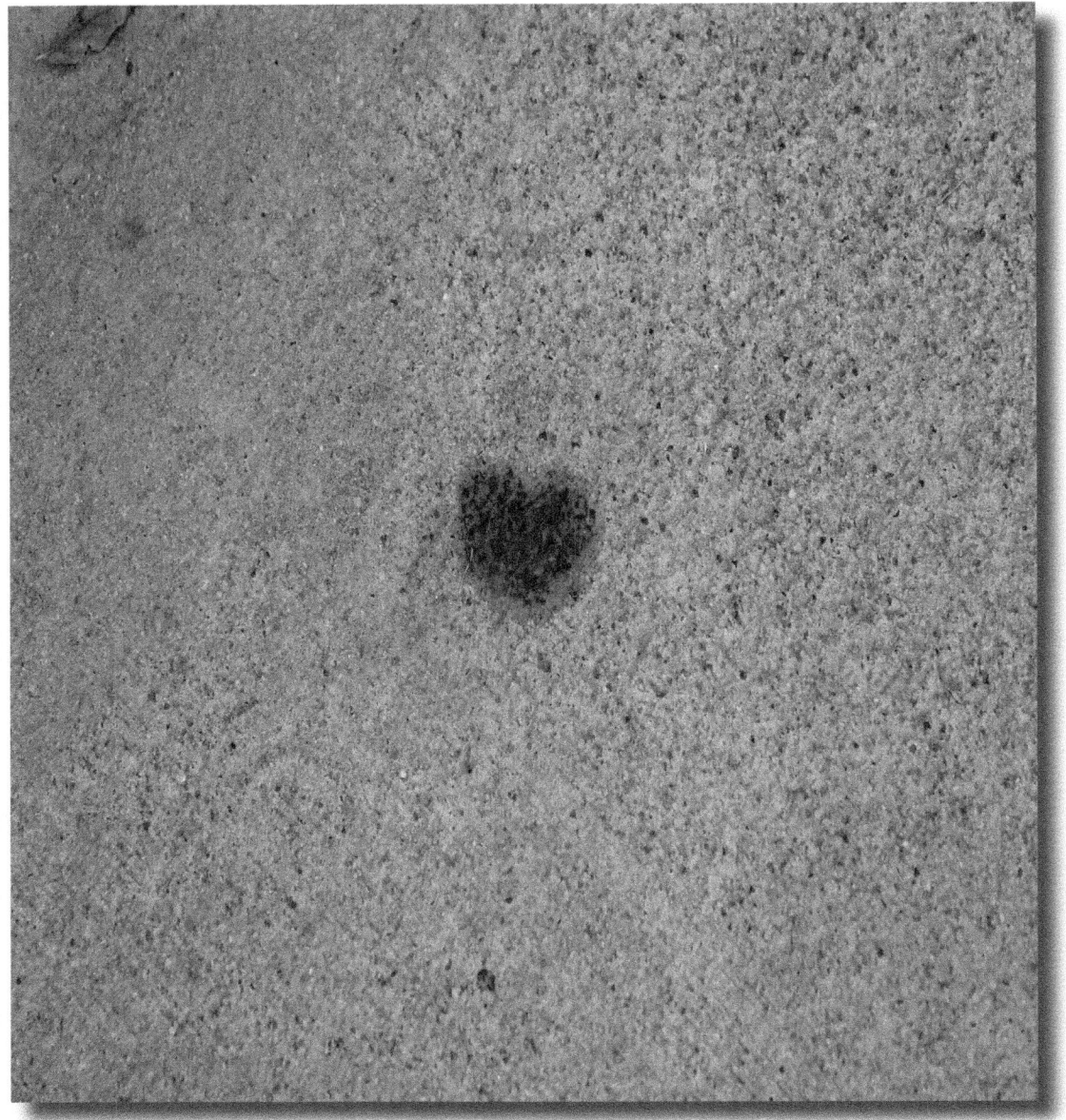

"When I despair, I remember that all through history the way of truth and love have always won. There have been tyrants and murderers, and for a time, they can seem invincible, but in the end, they always fall. Think of it...always."

~ Mahatma Gandhi

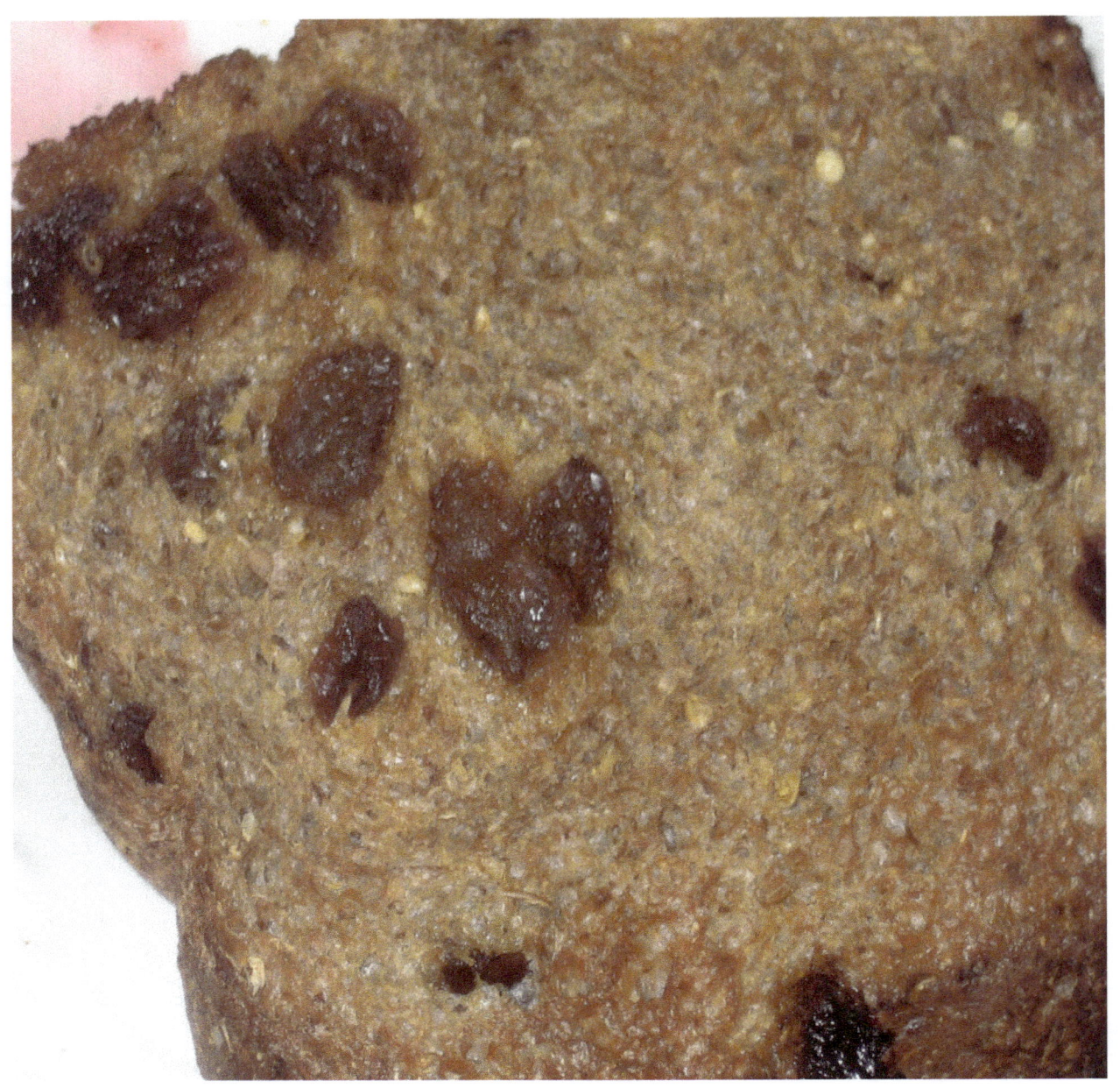

"I fell in love with her courage, her sincerity, and her flaming self respect. And it's these things I'd believe in, even if the whole world indulged in wild suspicions that she wasn't all she should be. I love her and it is the beginning of everything".

~F. Scott Fitzgerald

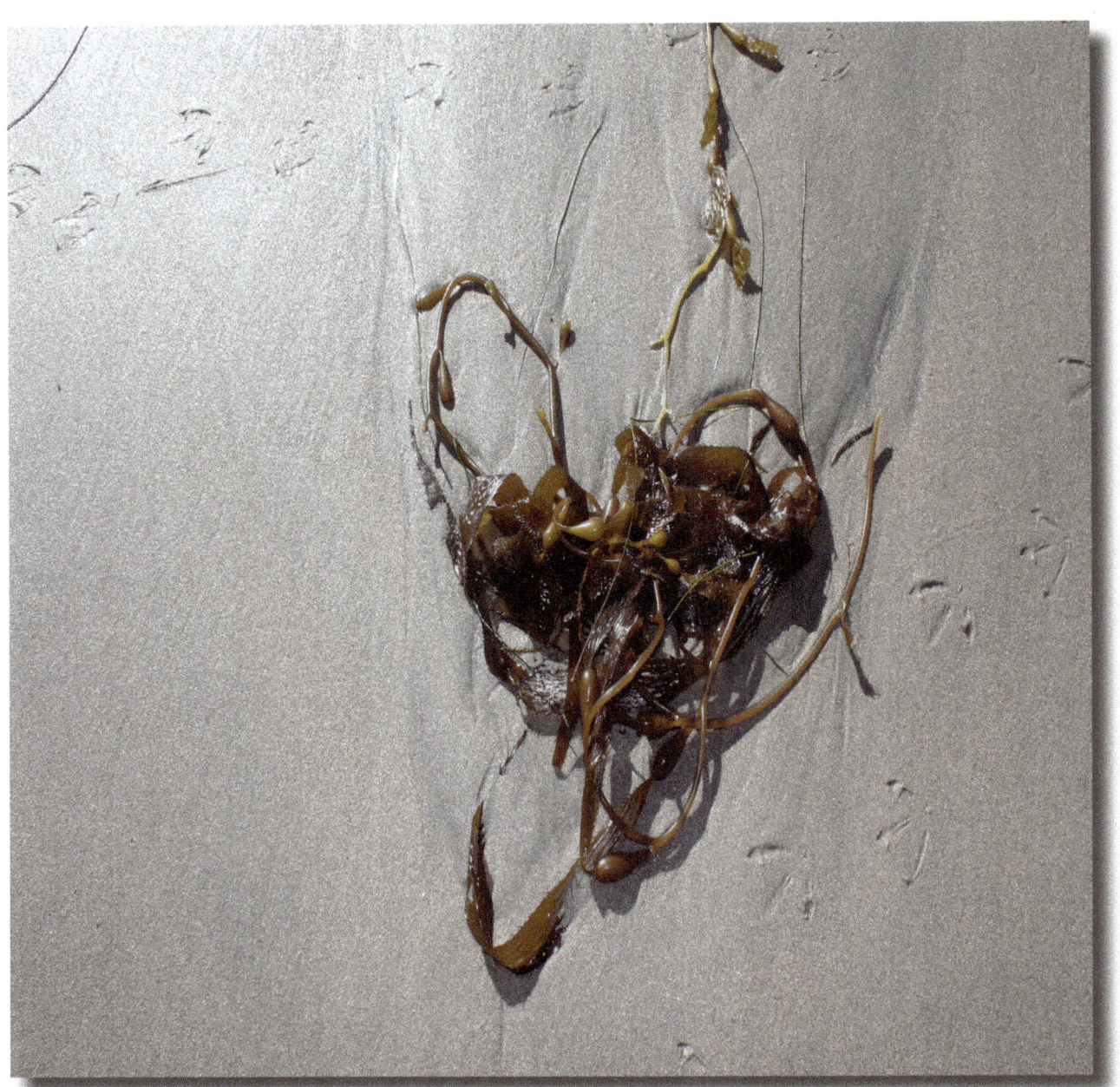

"A loving relationship is one in which the loved one is free to be himself – to laugh with me, but never at me; to cry with me, but never because of me; to love life, to love himself, to love being loved. Such a relationship is based upon freedom and can never grow in a jealous heart."

~ Leo F. Buscaglia

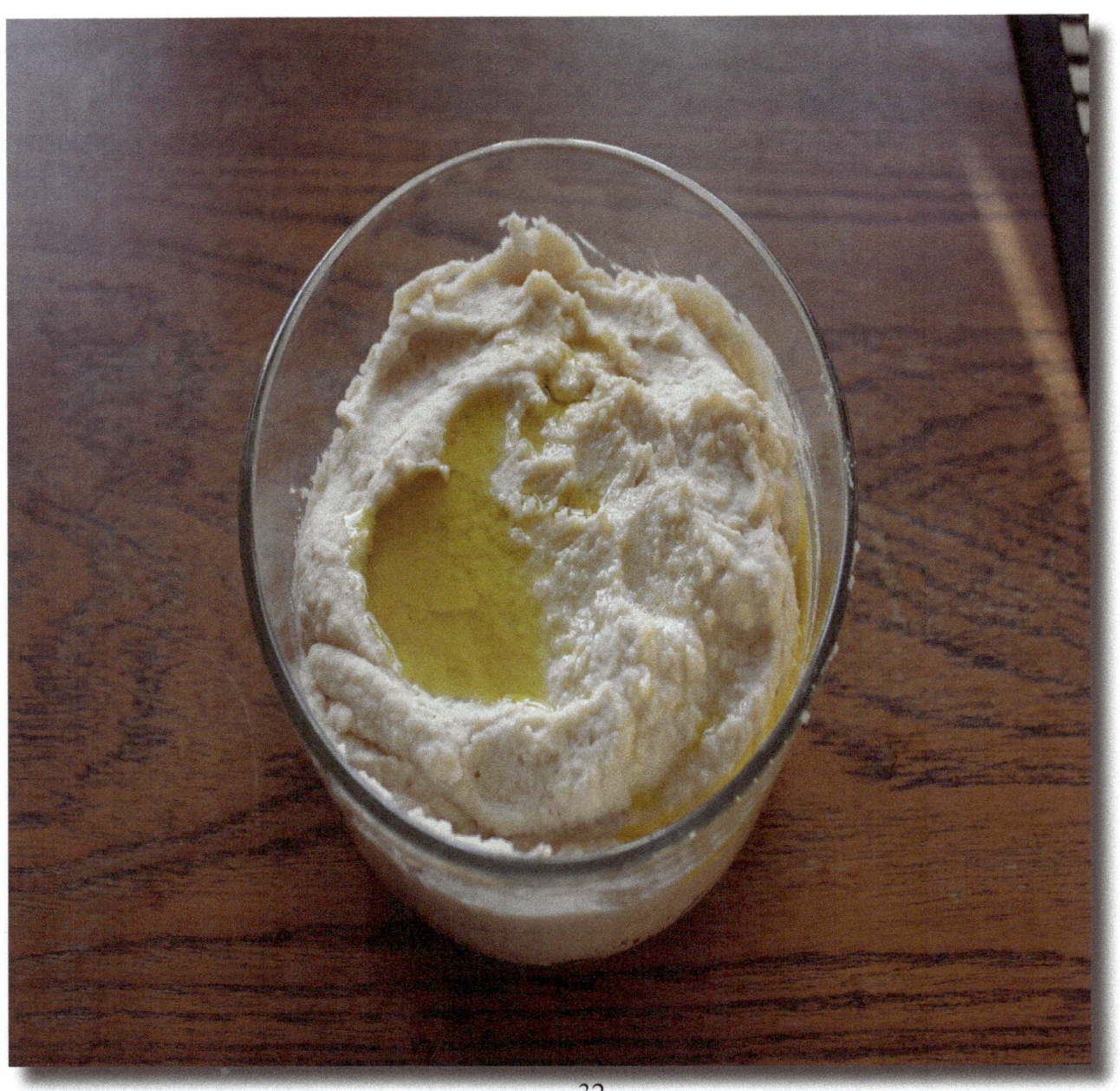

"And remember, as it was written, to love another person is to see the face of God."

~ Les Miserables

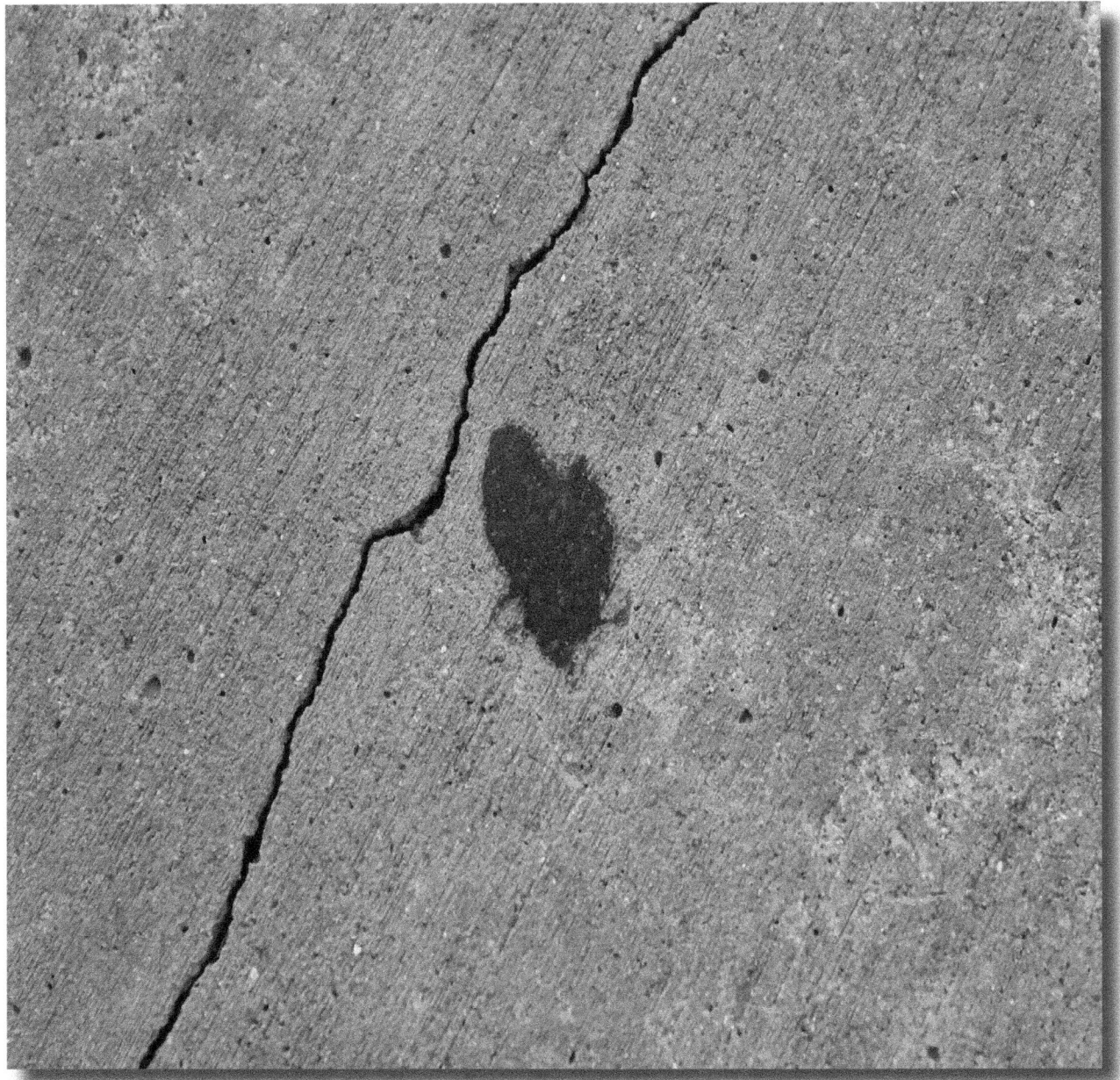

"I'm selfish, impatient and a little insecure. I make mistakes, I am out of control and at times hard to handle. But if you can't handle me at my worst, then you sure as hell don't deserve me at my best".

~Marilyn Monroe

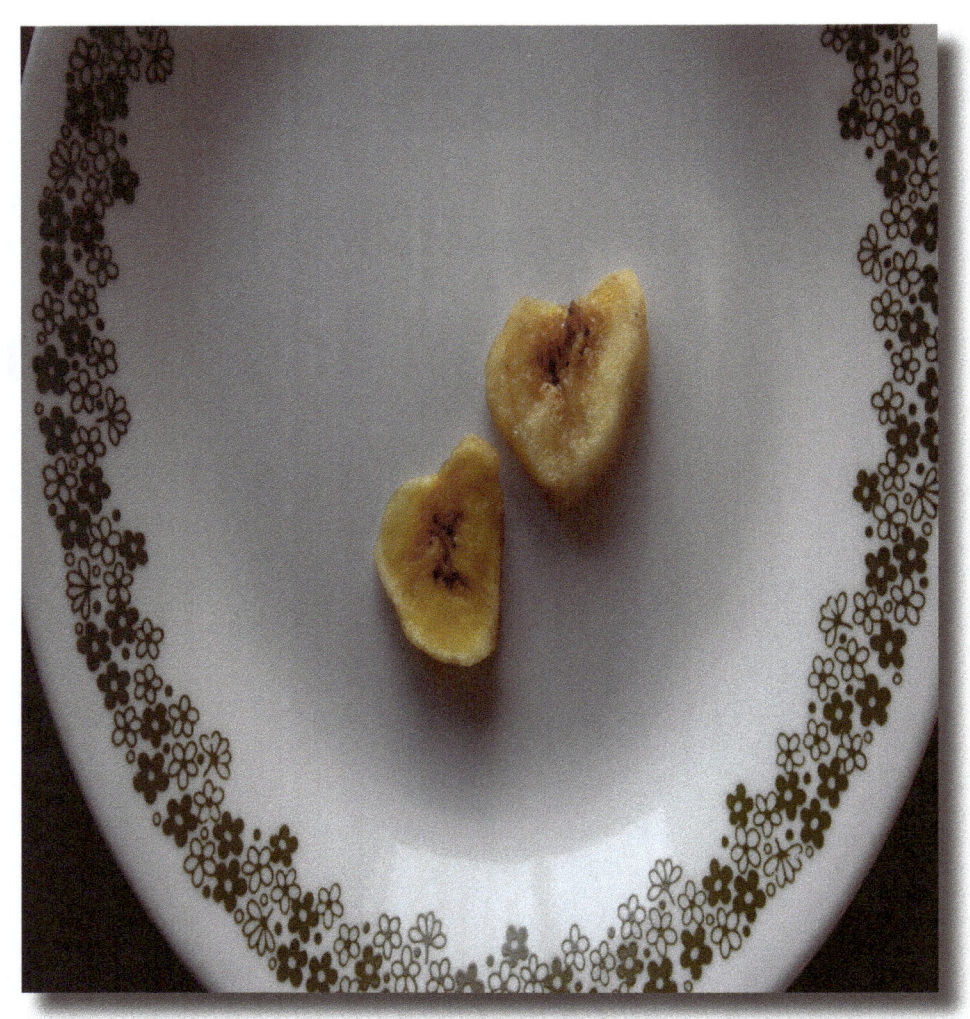

"When two people are meant for each other, no time is too long, no distance is too far, no one can ever tear them apart".

~Unknown

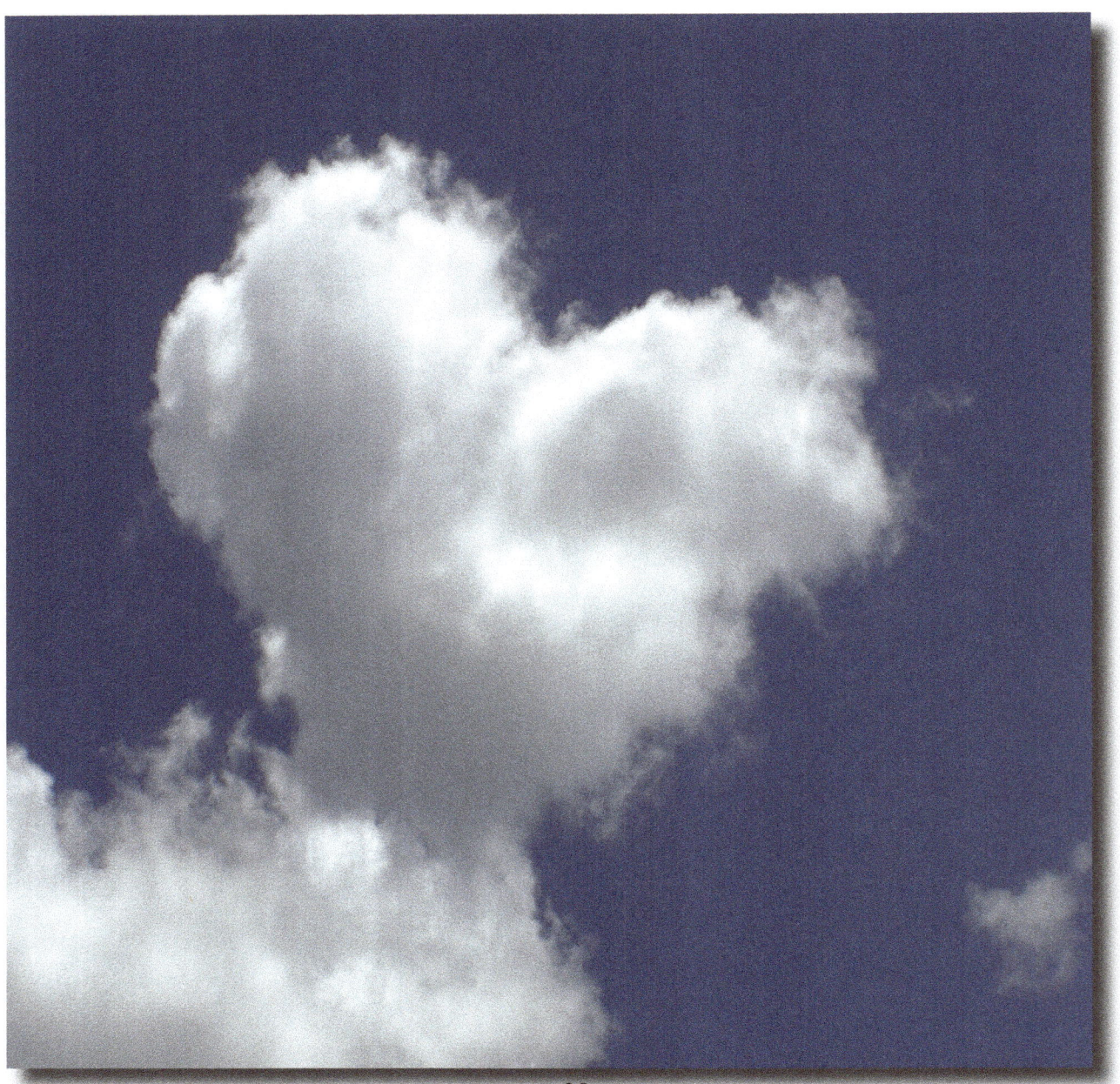

"Love is a promise; love is
a souvenir, once given never
forgotten, never let it disappear."

~ John Lennon

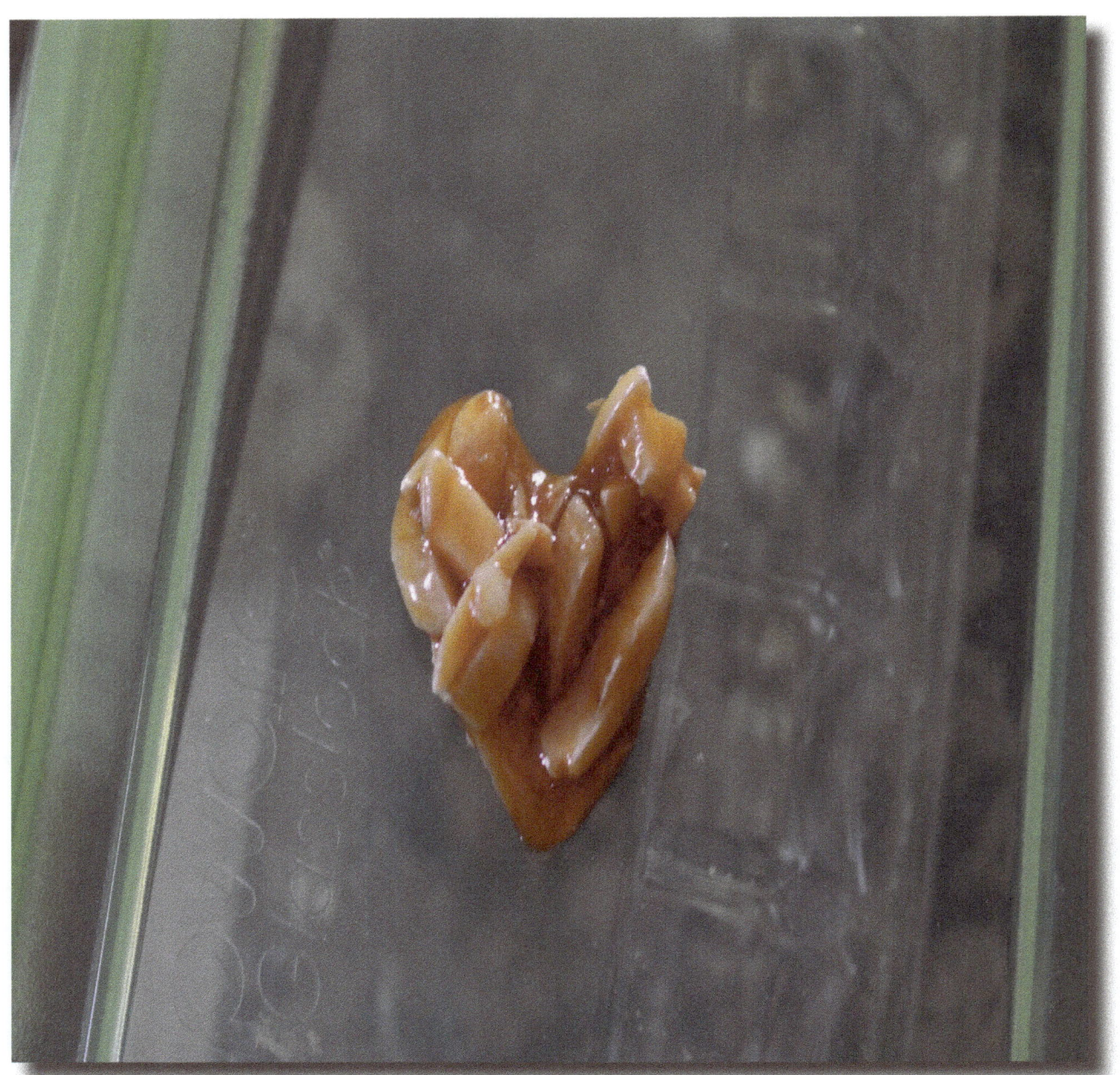

"I refuse to let what happened to me make me bitter. I still completely believe in love and I'm open to anything that will happen to me."

~ Nicole Kidman

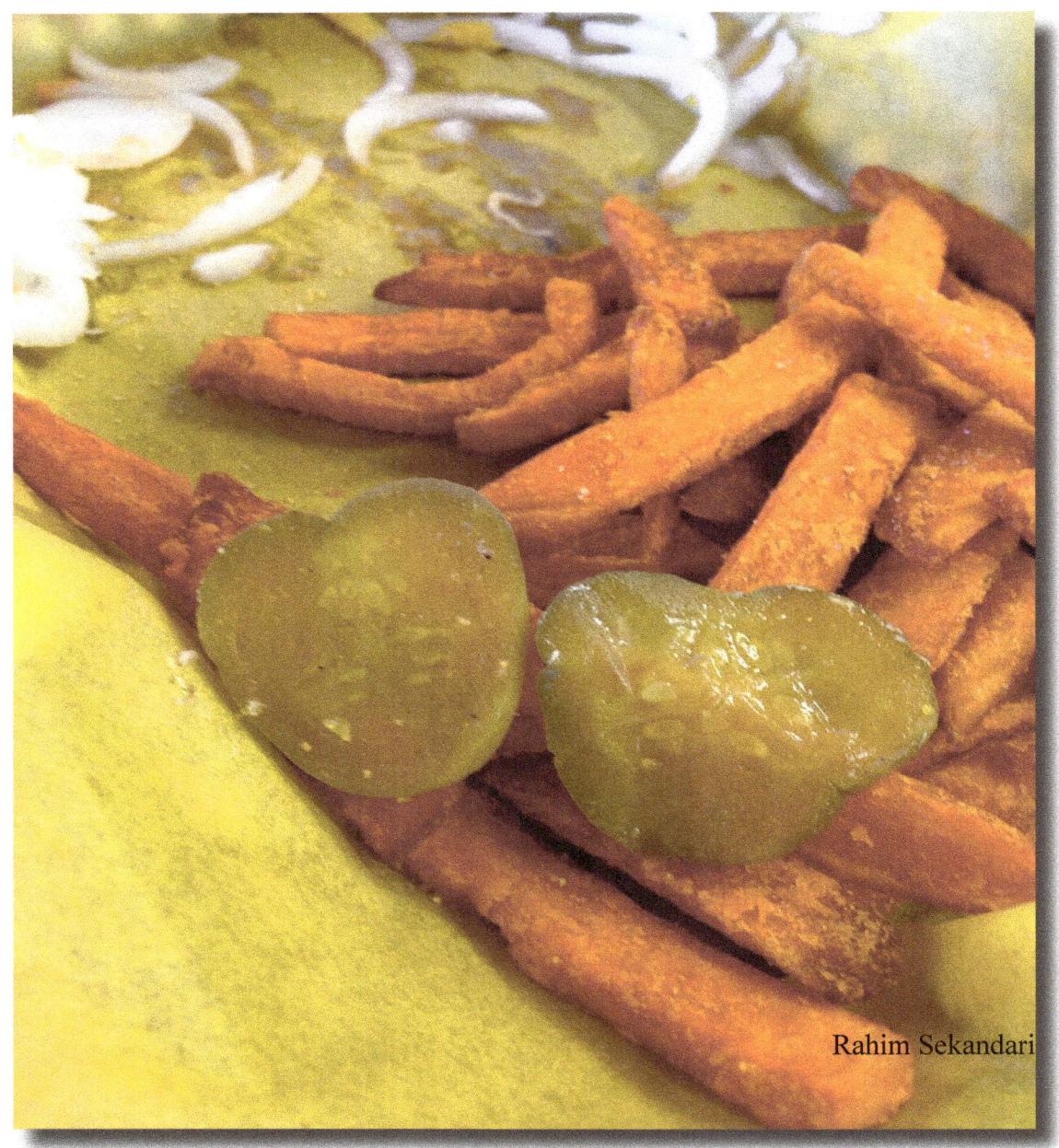

Rahim Sekandari

"The best love is the kind that awakens the soul; that makes us reach for more, that plants the fire in our hearts and brings peace to our minds. That's what I hope to give you forever."

~ The Notebook

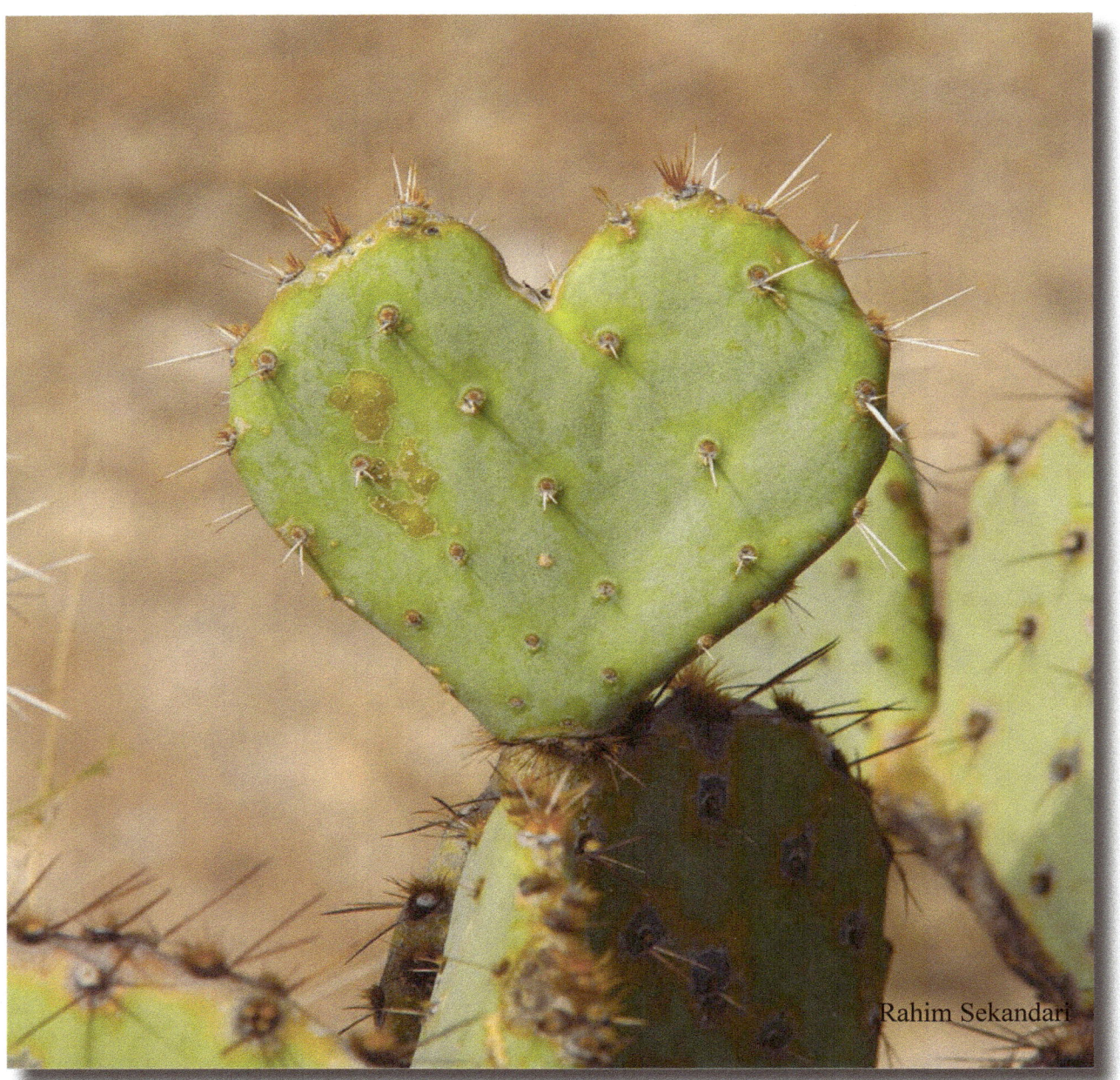

Rahim Sekandari

"There is no remedy for love,
but to love more."

~ Thoreau

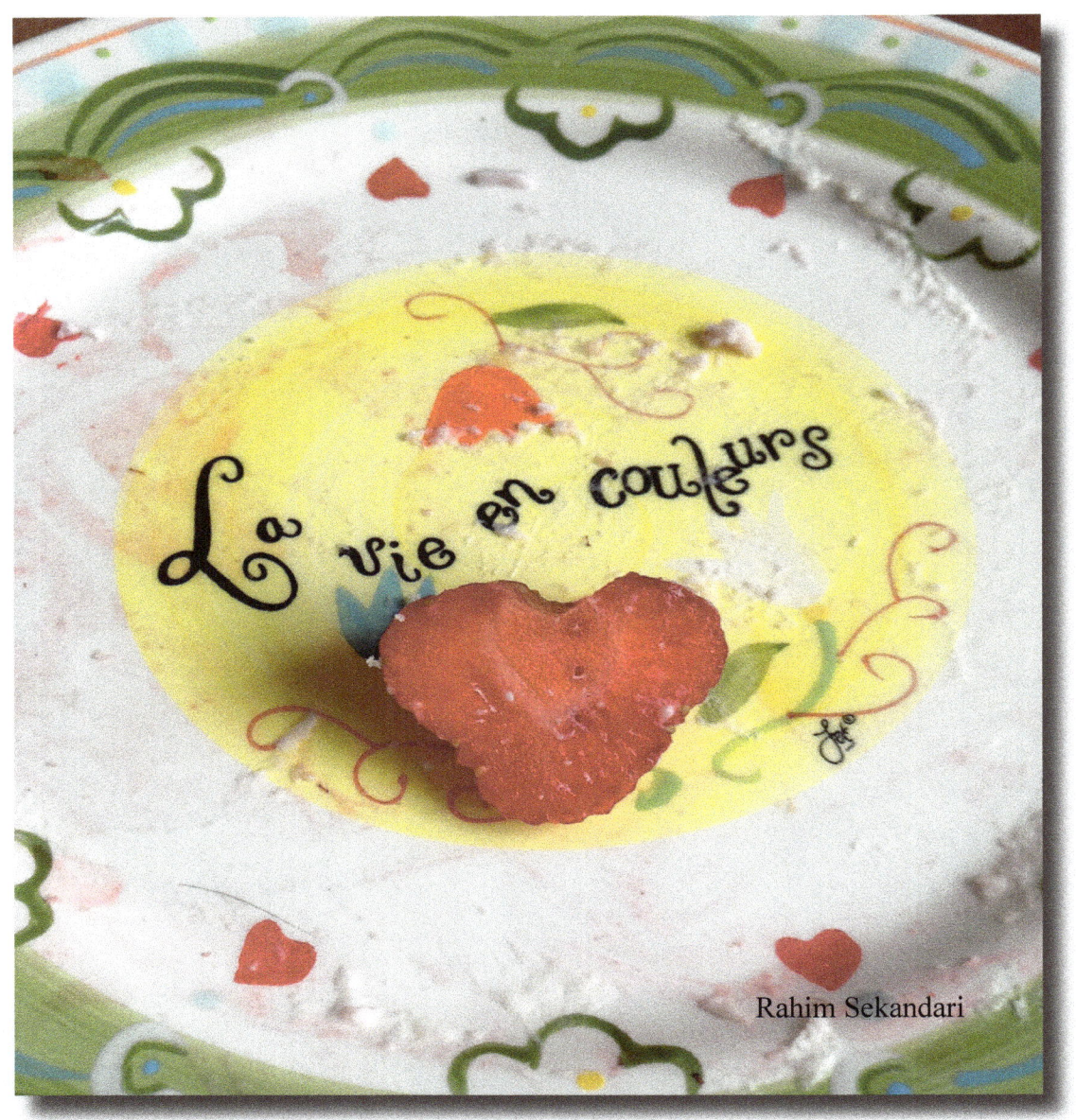

La vie en couleurs

Rahim Sekandari

"Love is an emotion experienced by the many and enjoyed by the few."
~ Unknown

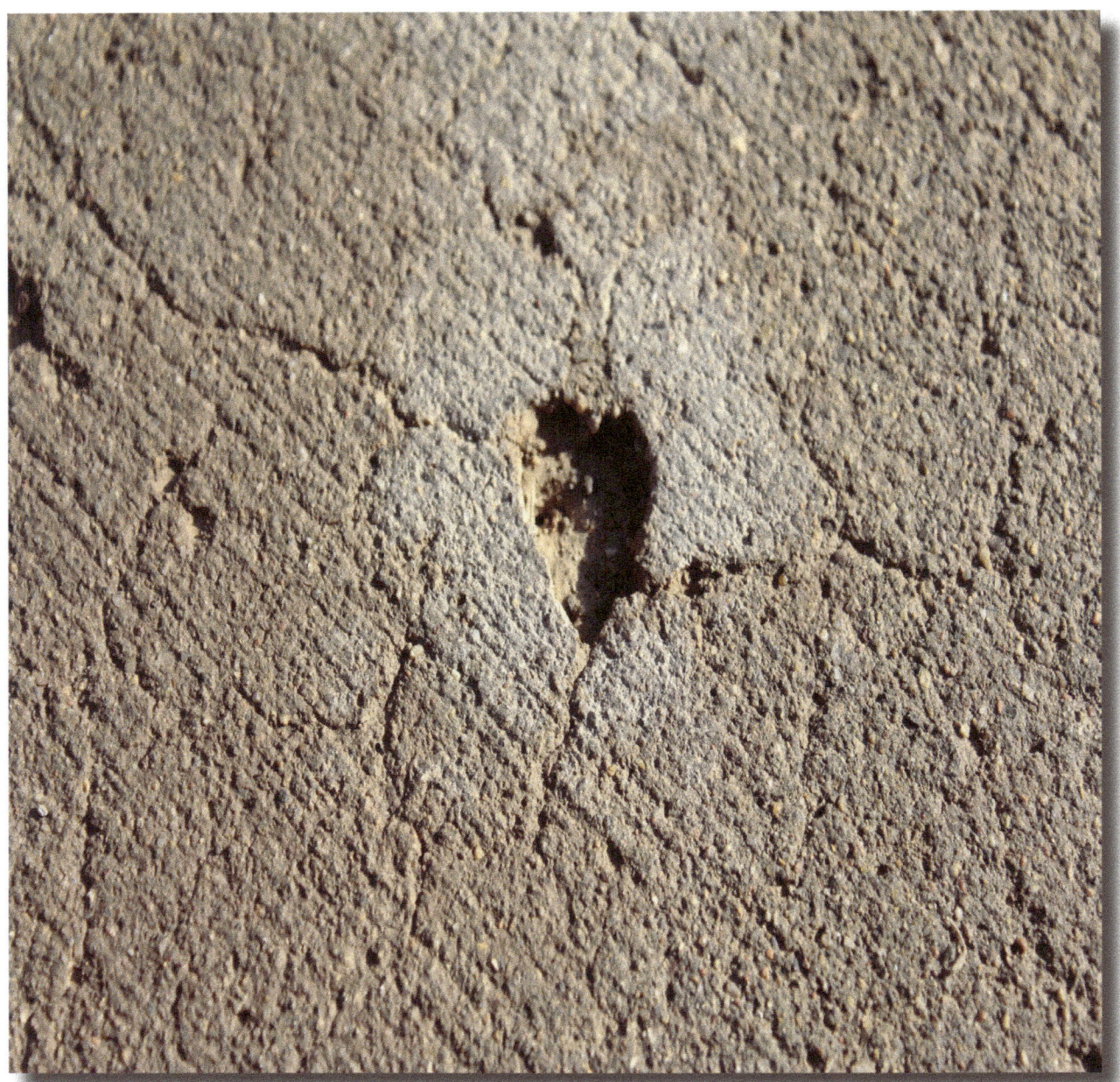

"Better to have lost and loved than never to have loved at all."

~ Hemingway

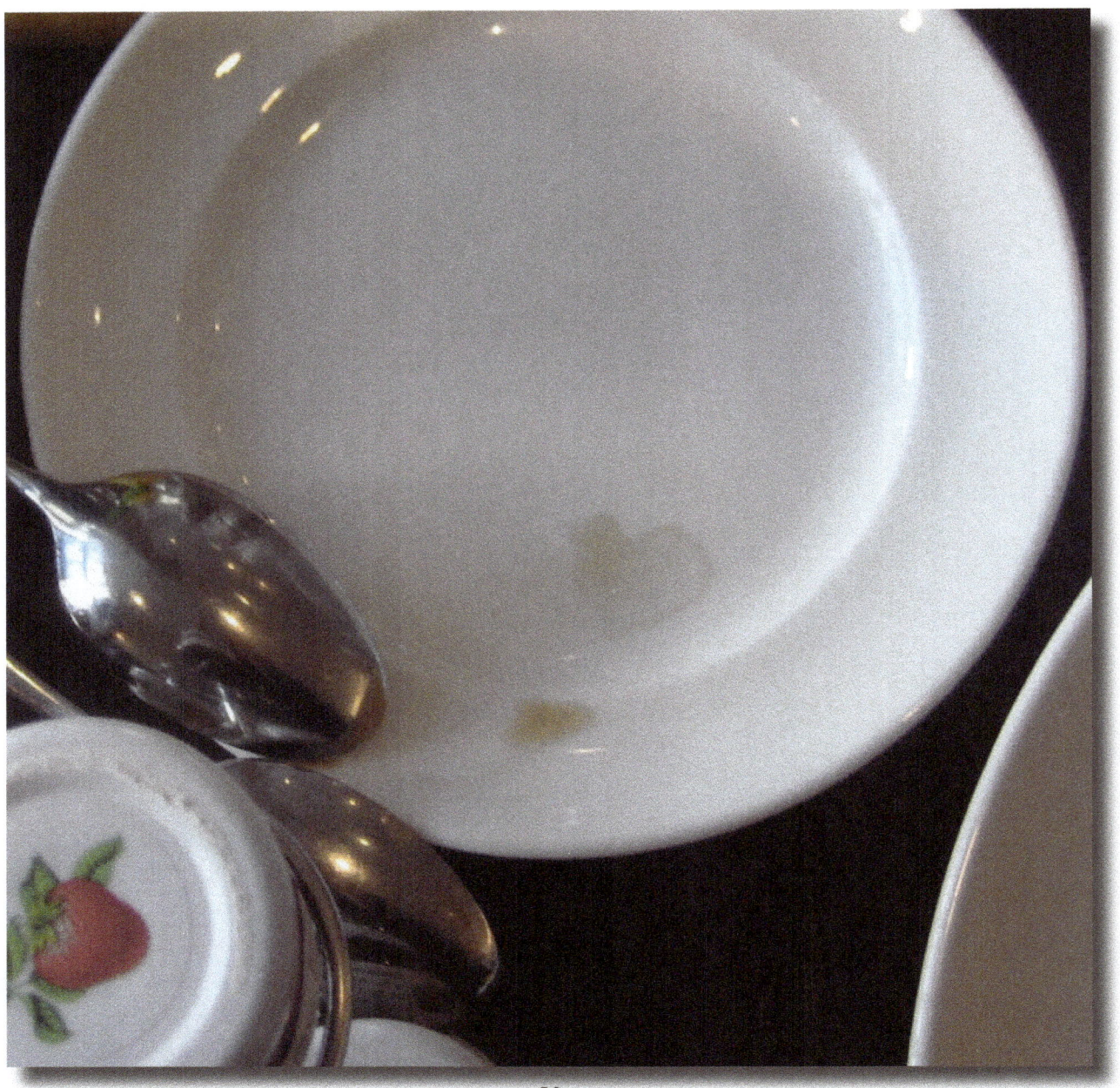

"You don't marry someone you can live with – you marry the person who you cannot live without."

~Unknown

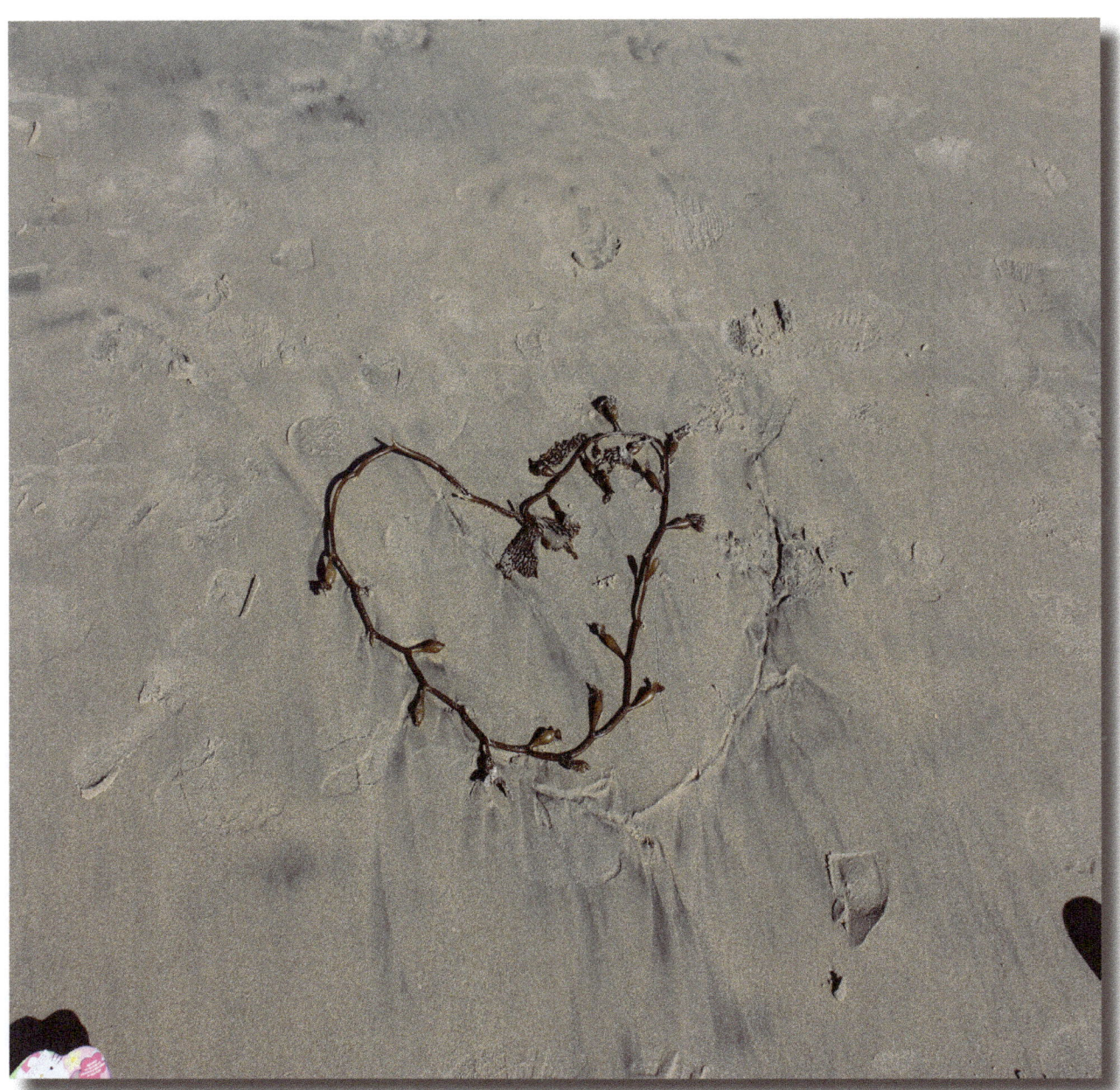

"The greater your capacity to love, the greater your capacity to feel the pain."

~ Jennifer Aniston

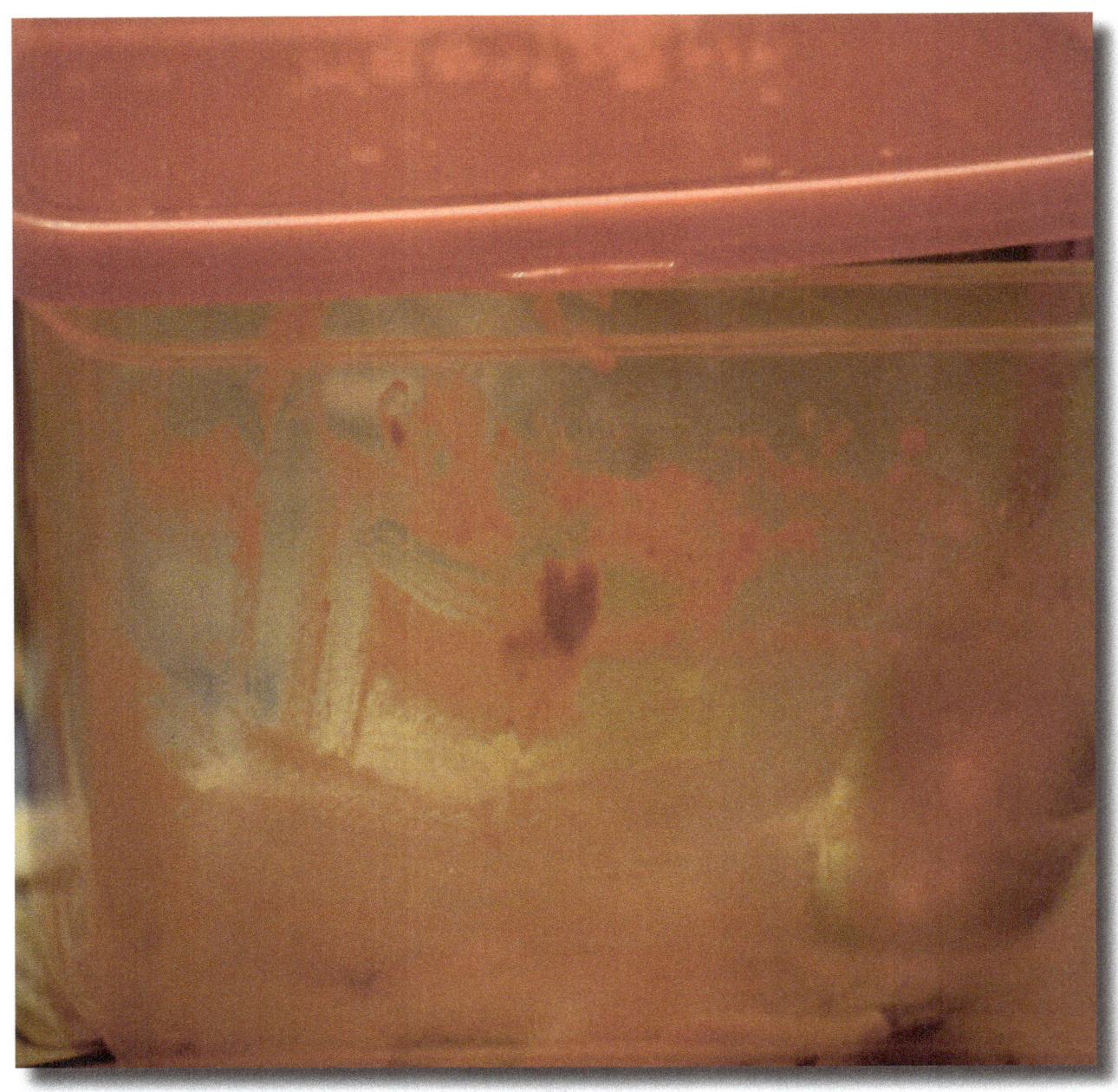

"The greatest happiness of life is the conviction that we are loved; loved for ourselves, or rather, loved in spite of ourselves."

~ Victor Hugo

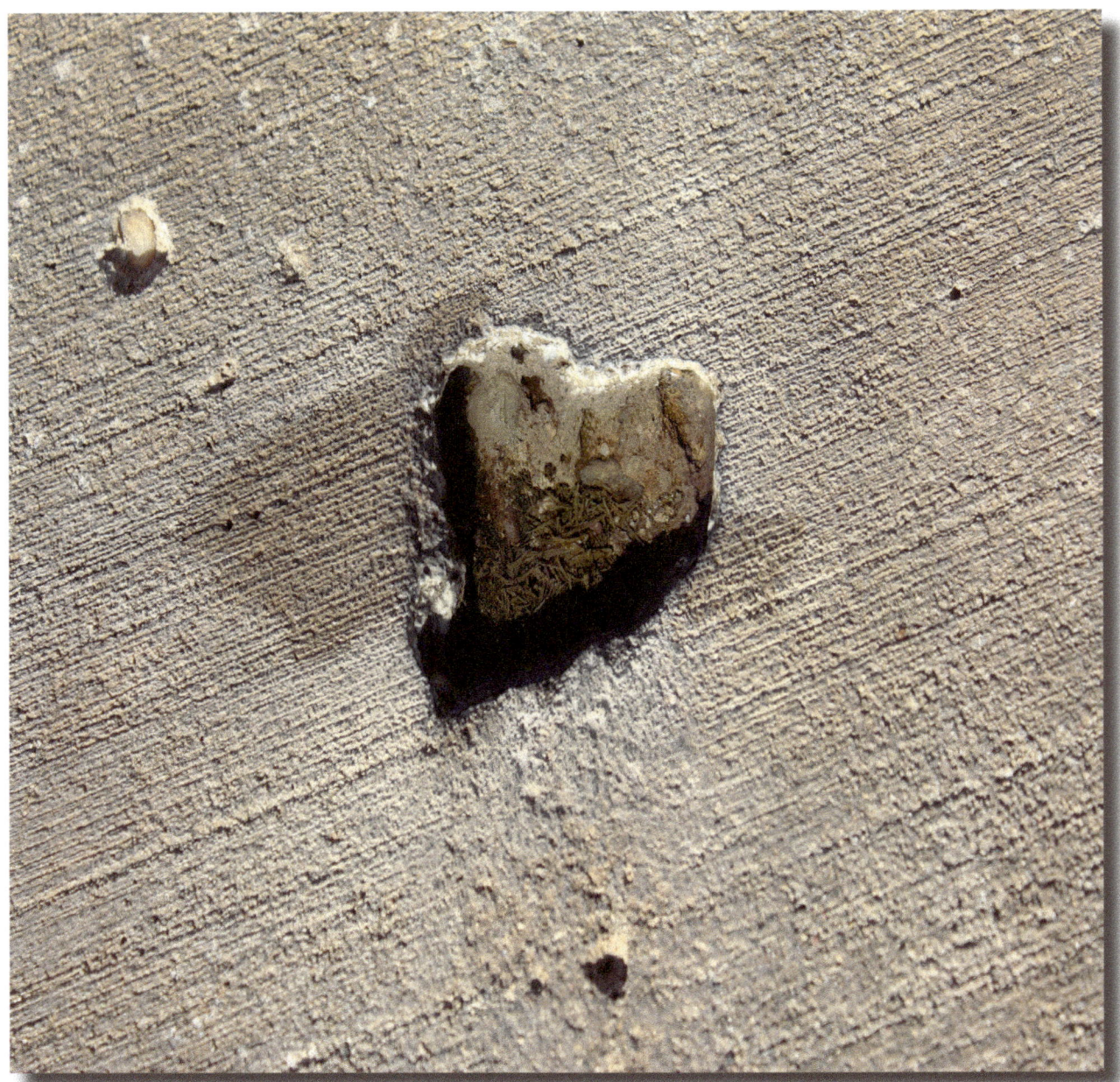

"With love, one can live even without happiness."

~ Fyodor Dostoyevsky

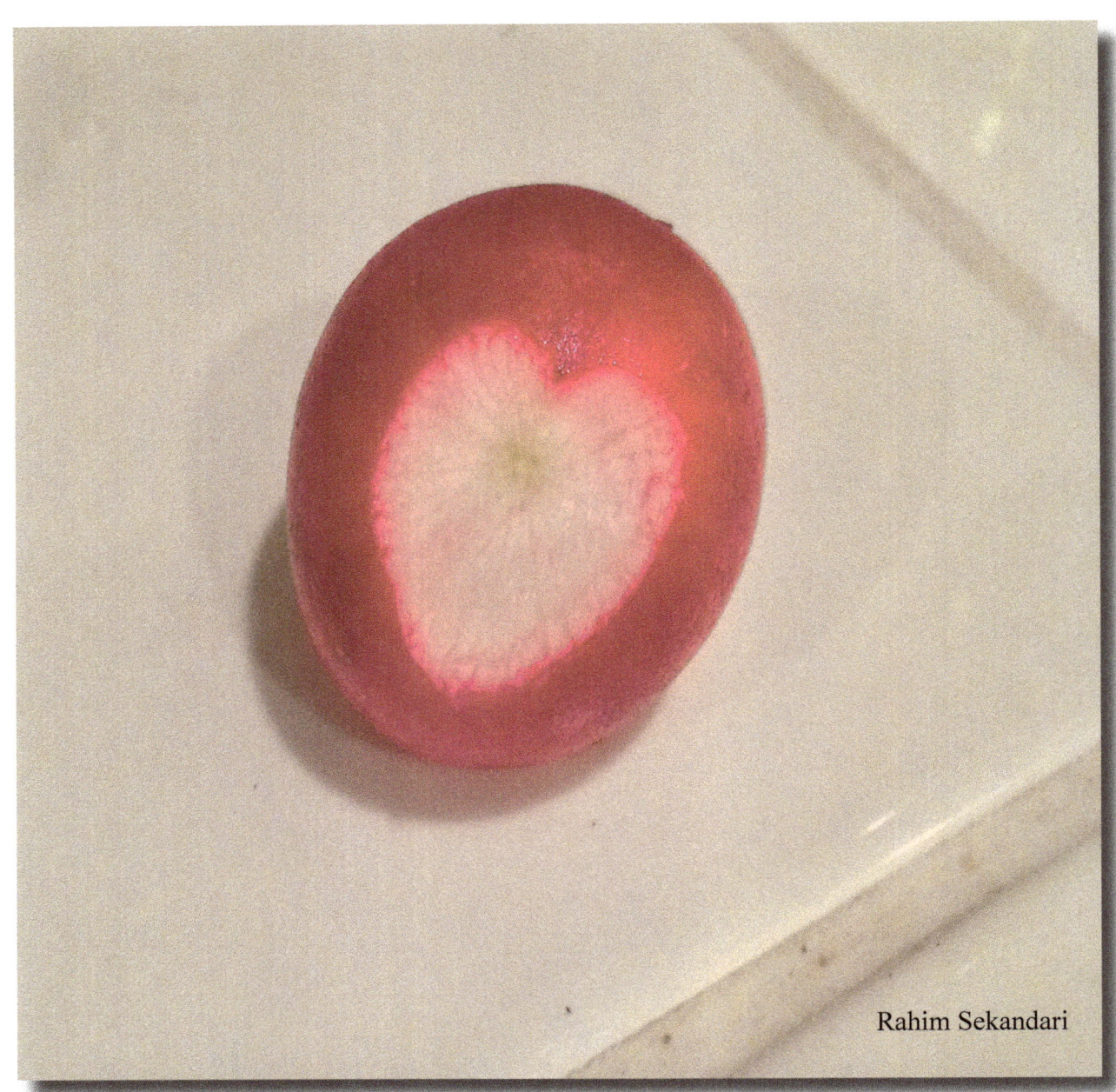

Rahim Sekandari

"Love cures people, both the ones who give it and the ones who receive it."

~ Dr. Karl Menninger

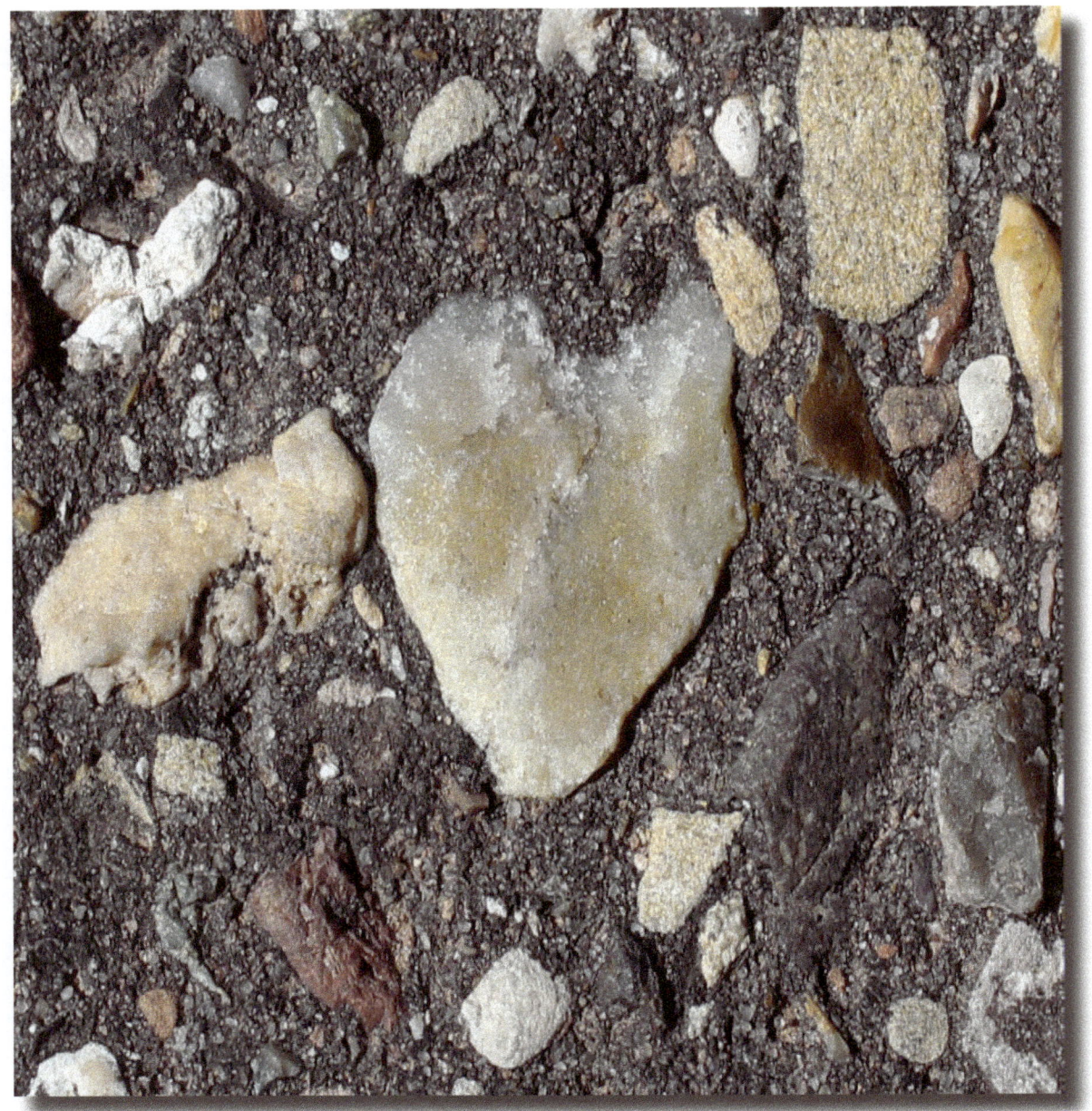

"The greatest thing you'll ever learn is to love and be loved in return."

~Nat King Cole

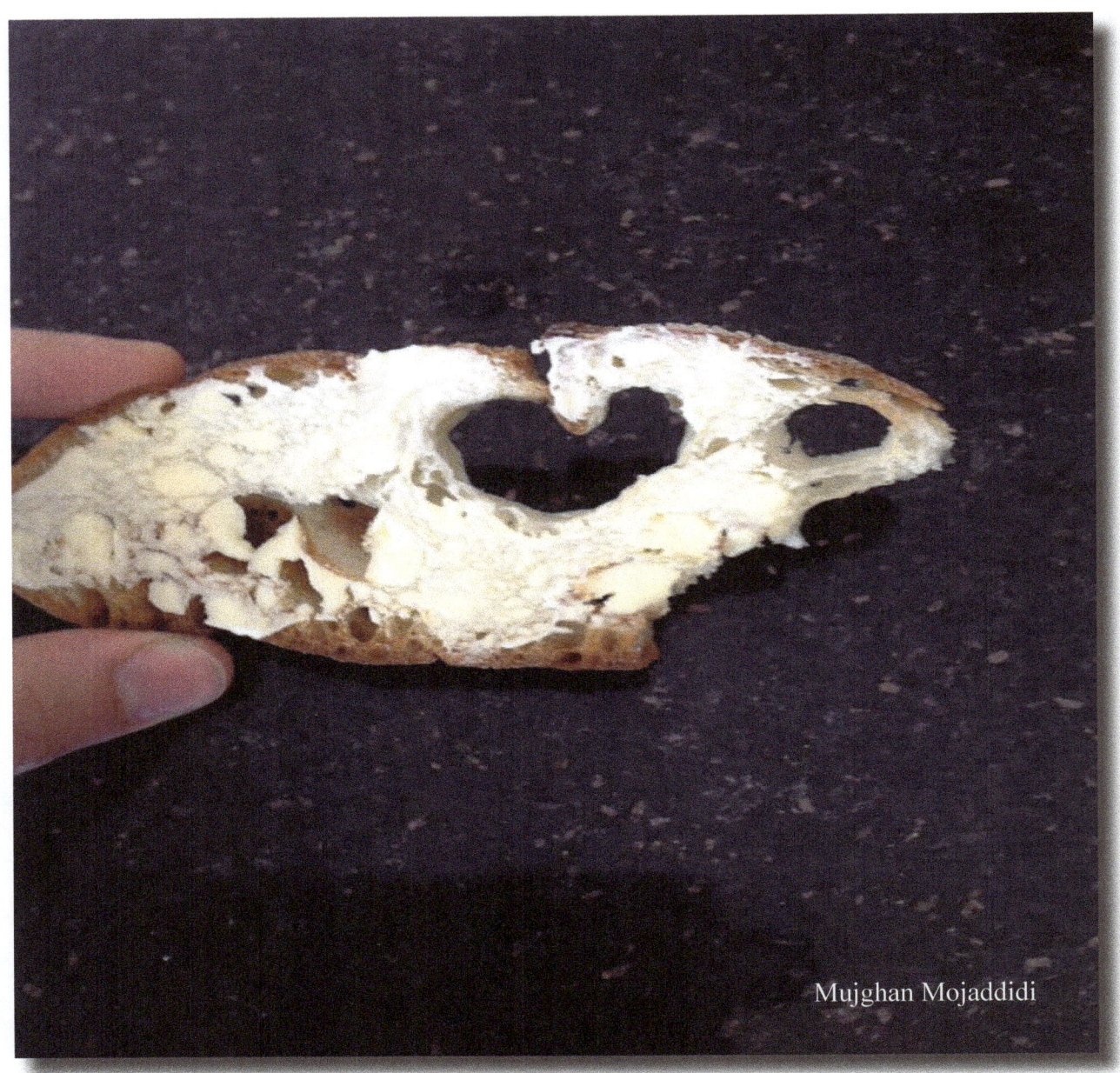

Mujghan Mojaddidi

"And in the end, the love you take, is equal to the love you make."

~ Paul McCartney

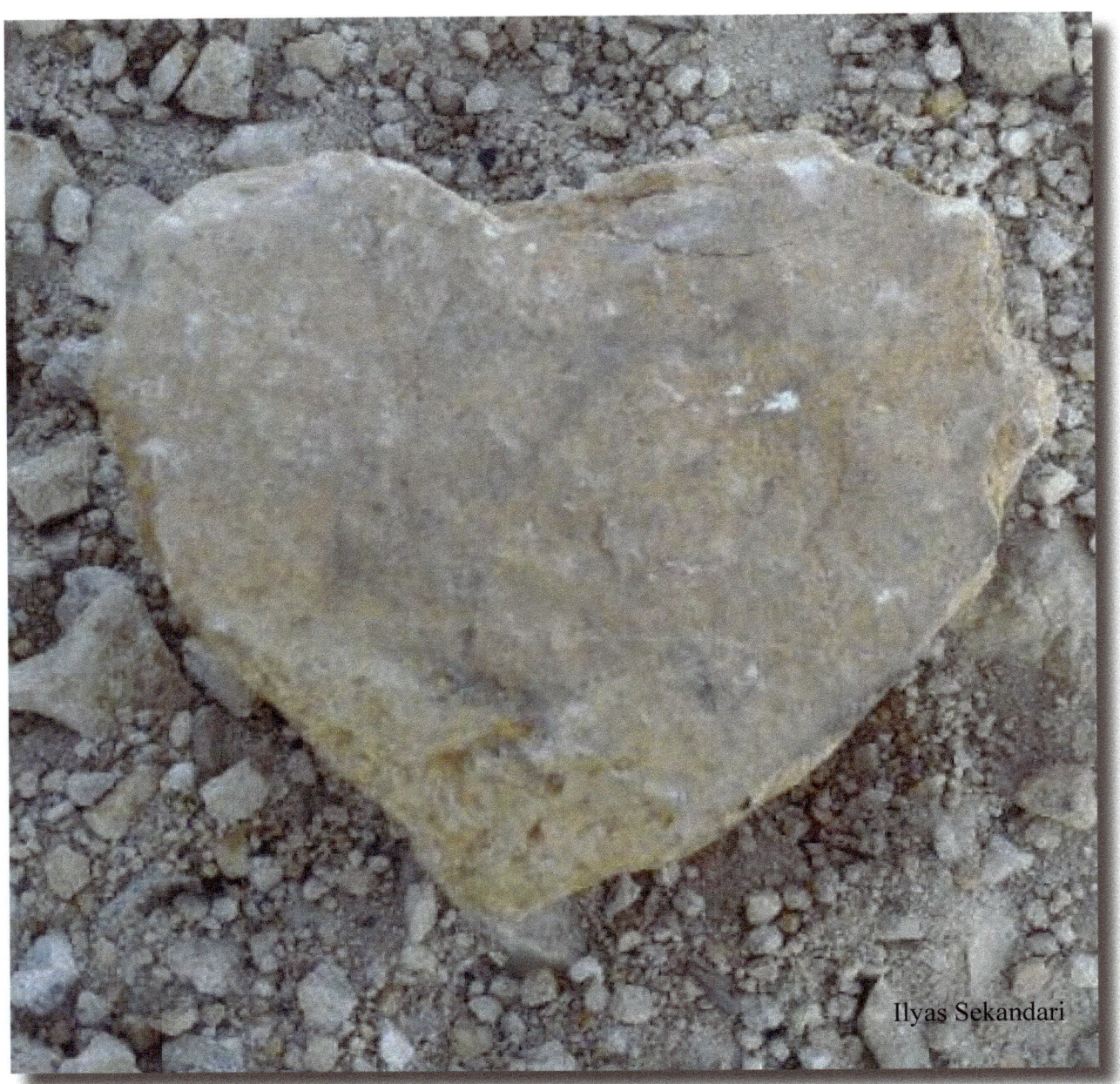

Ilyas Sekandari

"Don't settle for a relationship that won't let you be yourself."

~Oprah Winfrey

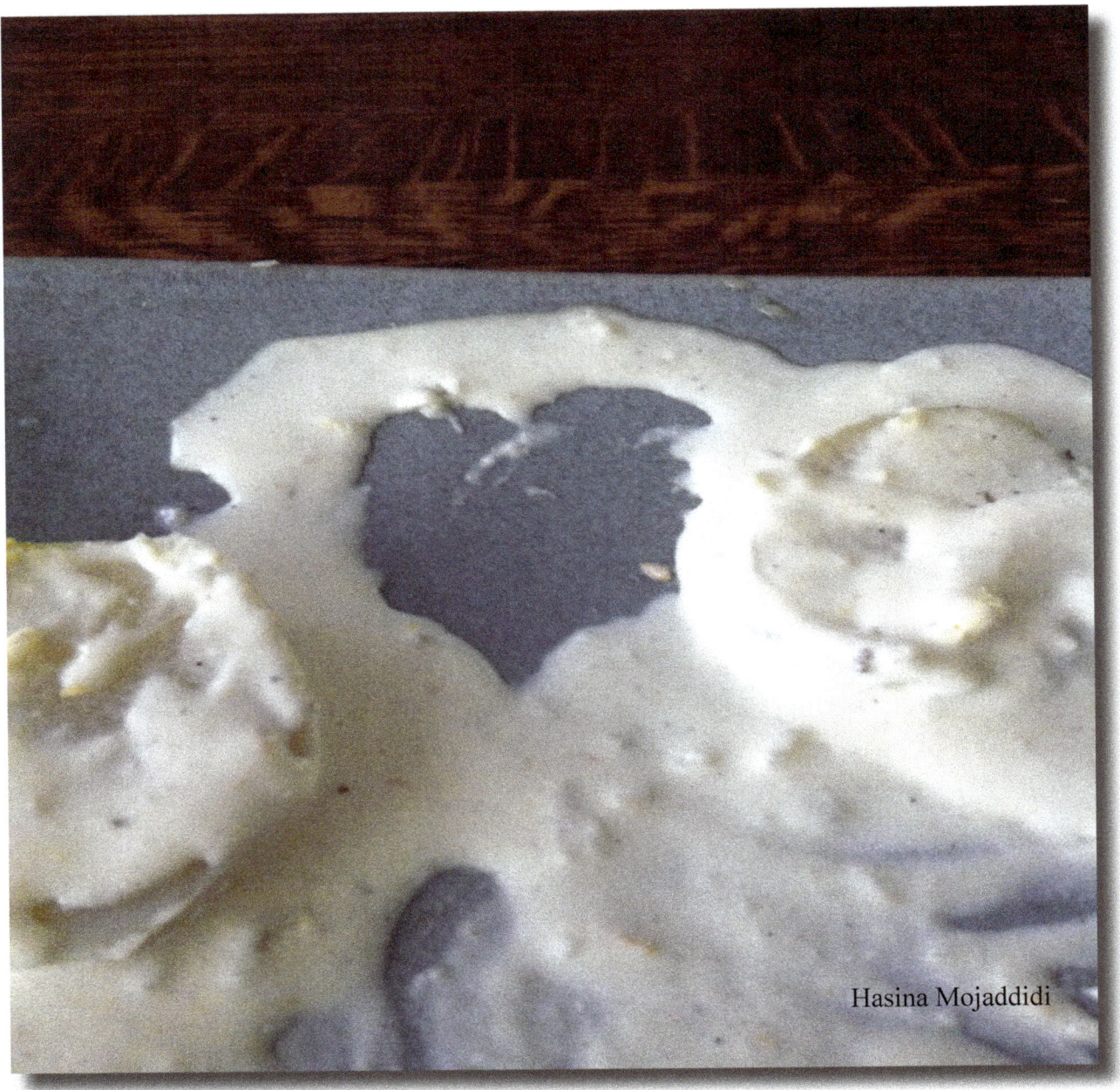

Hasina Mojaddidi

"You don't love someone because they're perfect, you love them in spite of the fact that they're not".

~ Jodi Picoult

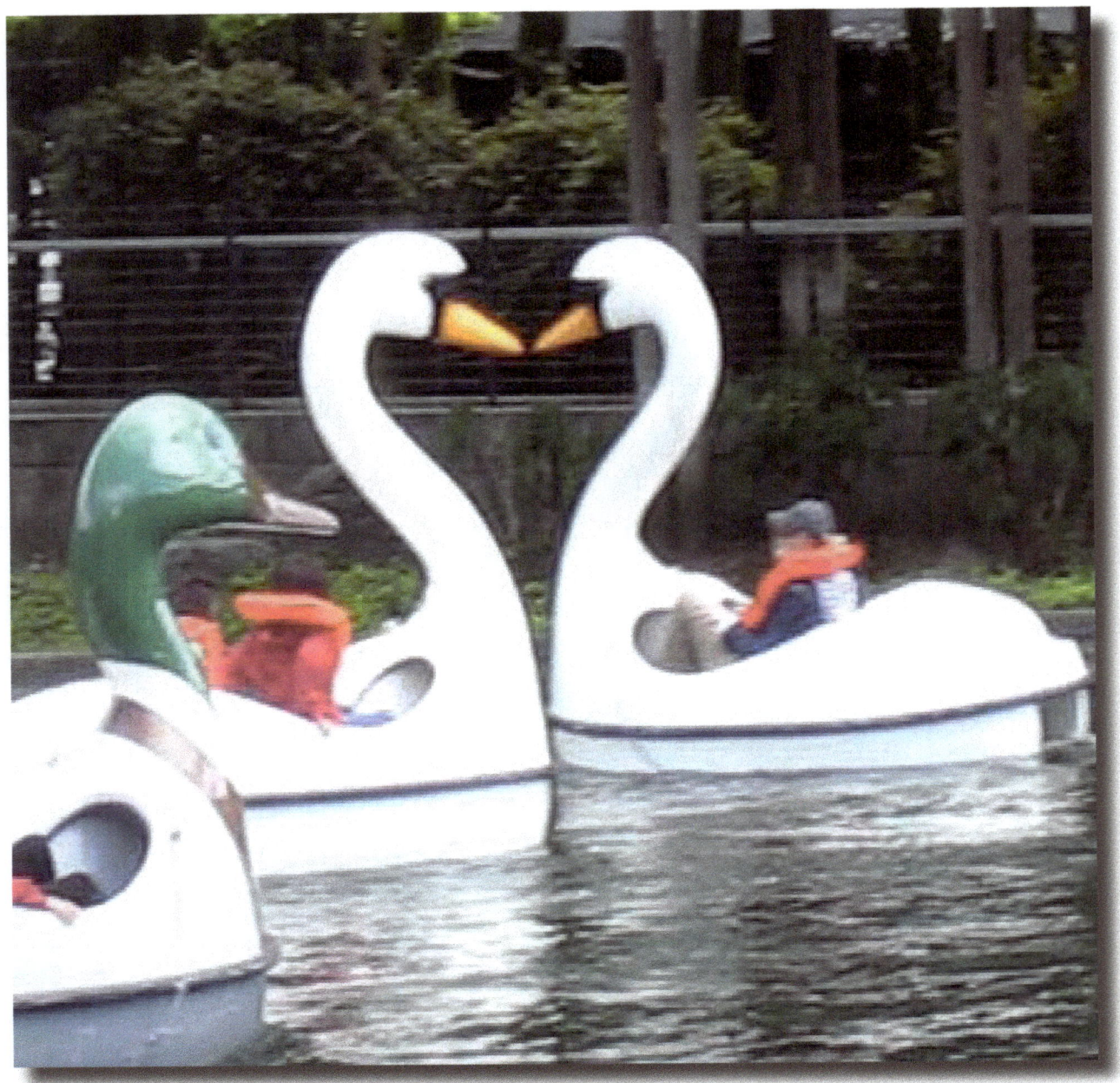

"Everyone says that loves hurts, but that's not true. Loneliness hurts. Rejection hurts. Losing someone hurts. Everyone confuses these things with love but in reality, love is the only thing in this world that covers up all the pain and makes us feel wonderful again".

~Unknown

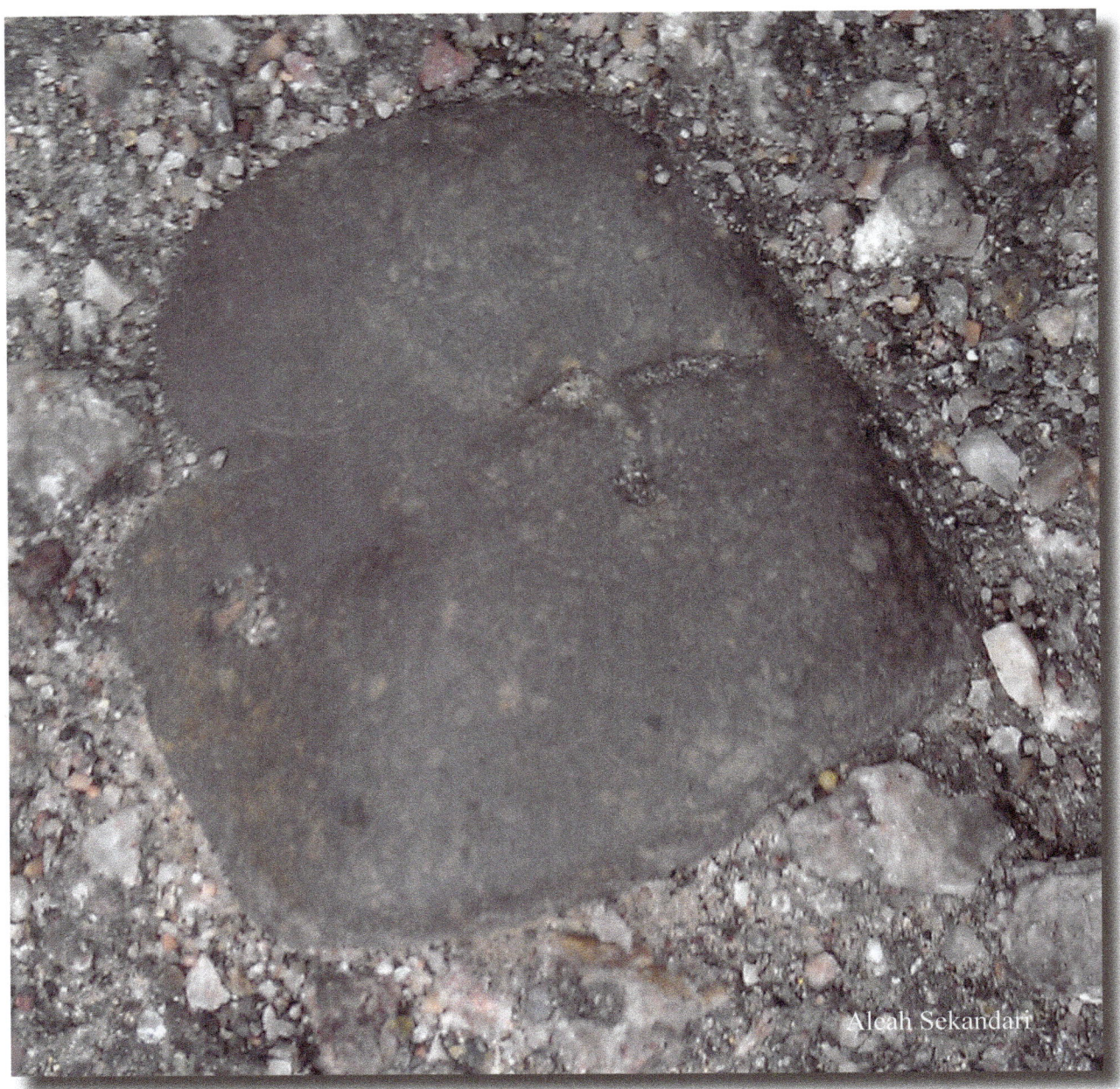

Aleah Sekandari

70

"It's not hard to find someone who tells you they love you, it's hard to find someone who actually means it".

~Unknown

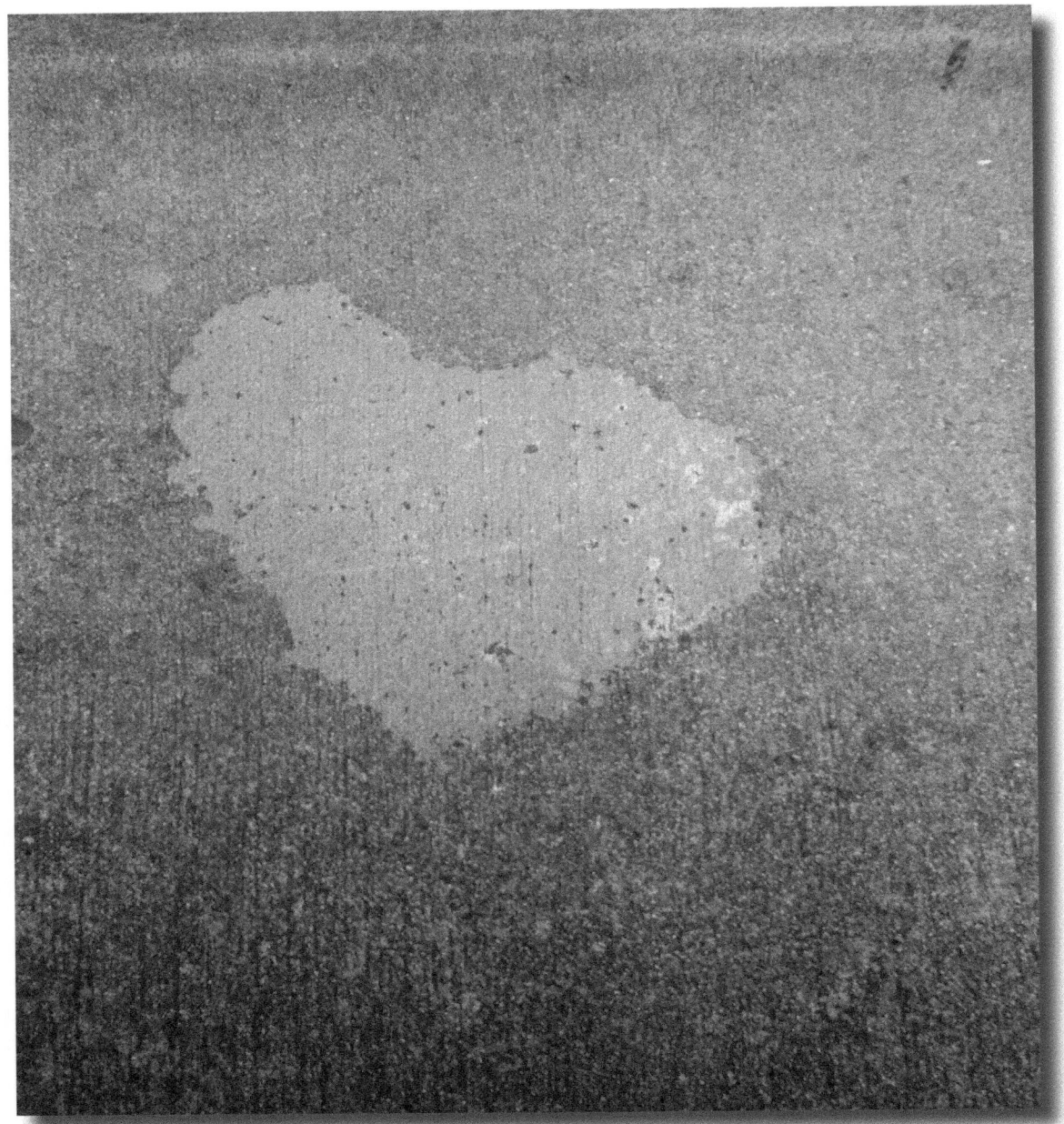

"The great tragedy of life is not that men perish, but that they cease to love"

~W. Somerset Maugham

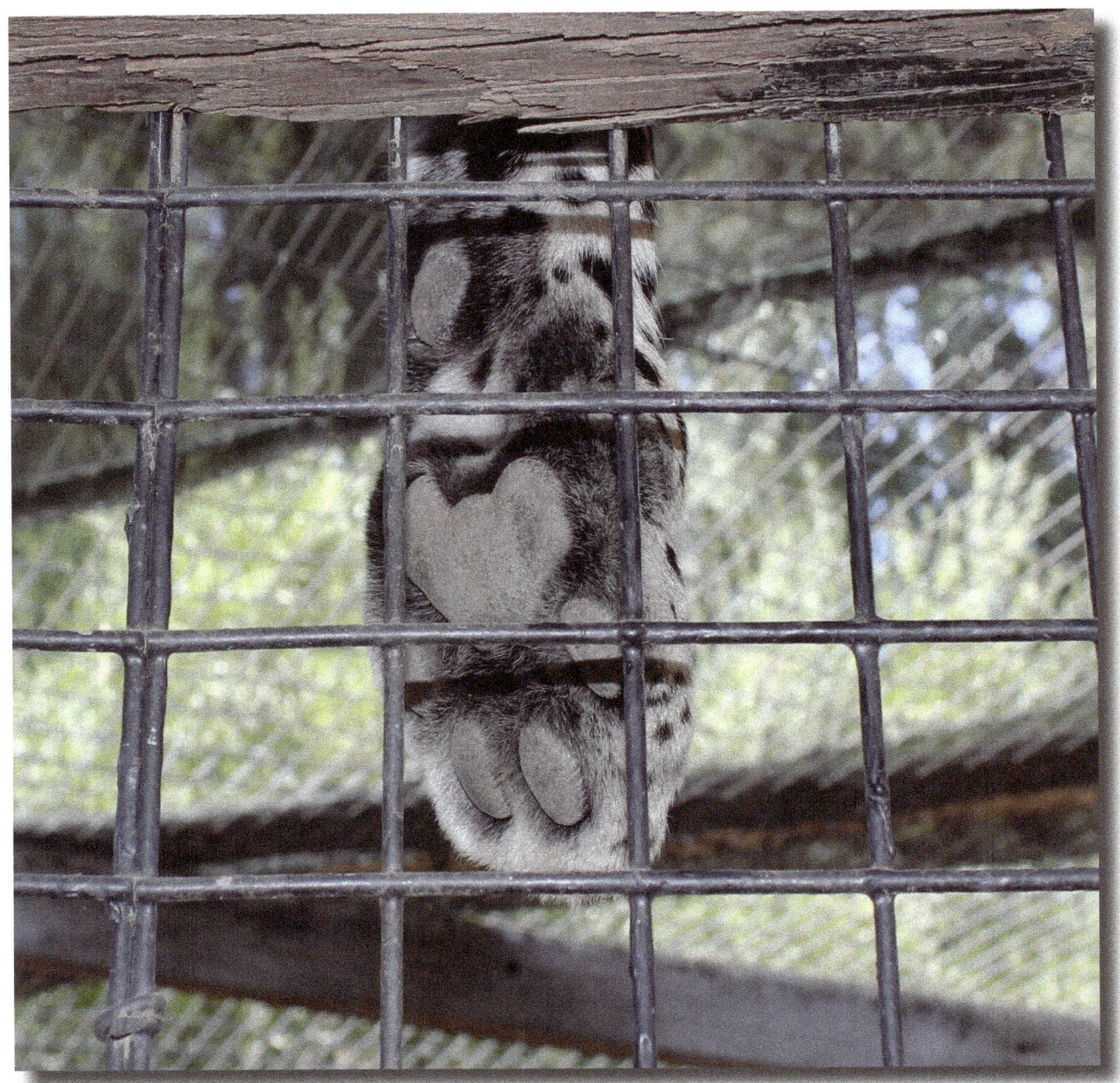

"You know it's love when all you want is that person to be happy, even if you're not part of their happiness."

~Julia Roberts

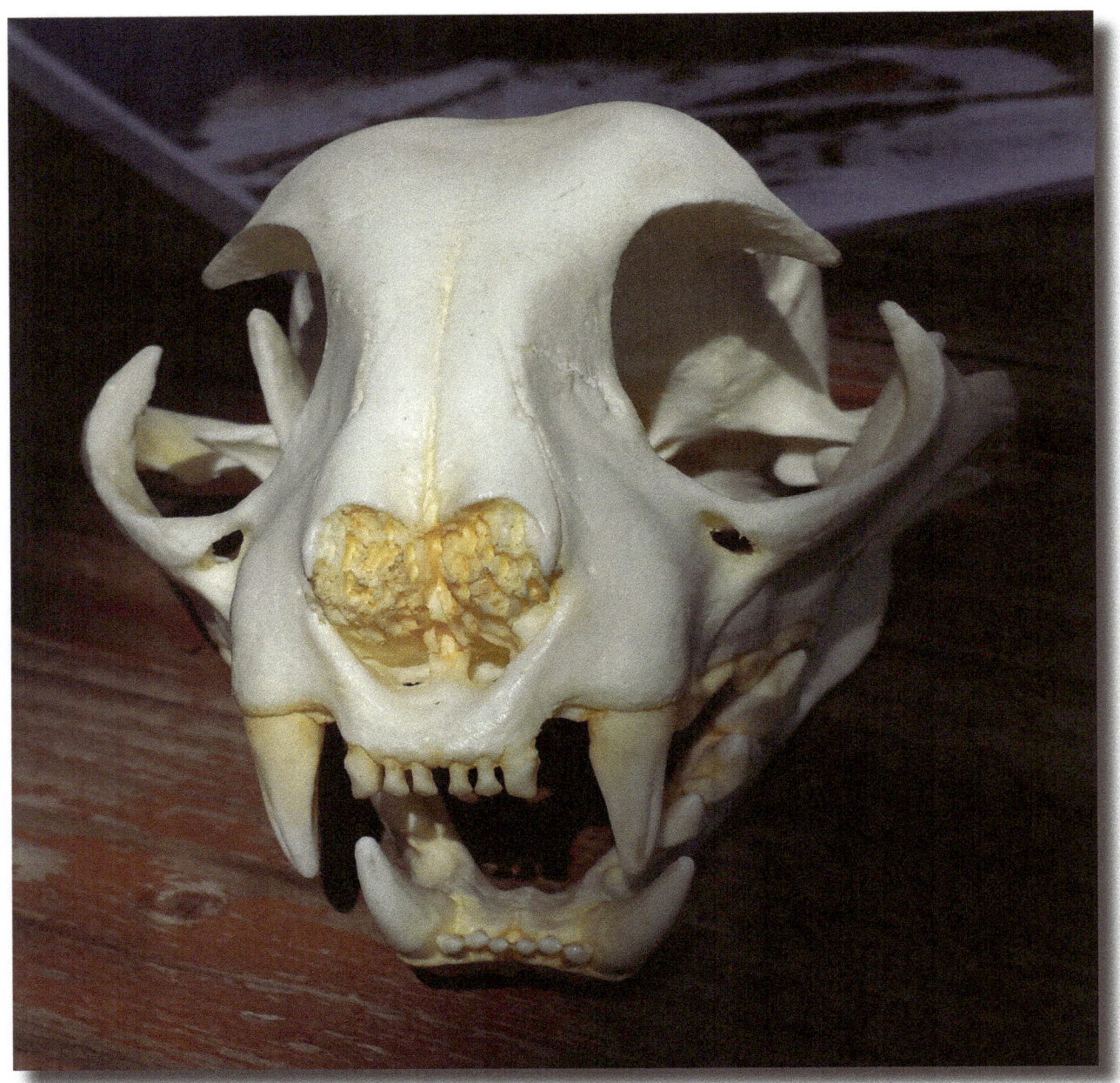

"The best and most beautiful things in this world cannot be seen or even heard, but must be felt with the heart."

~Helen Keller

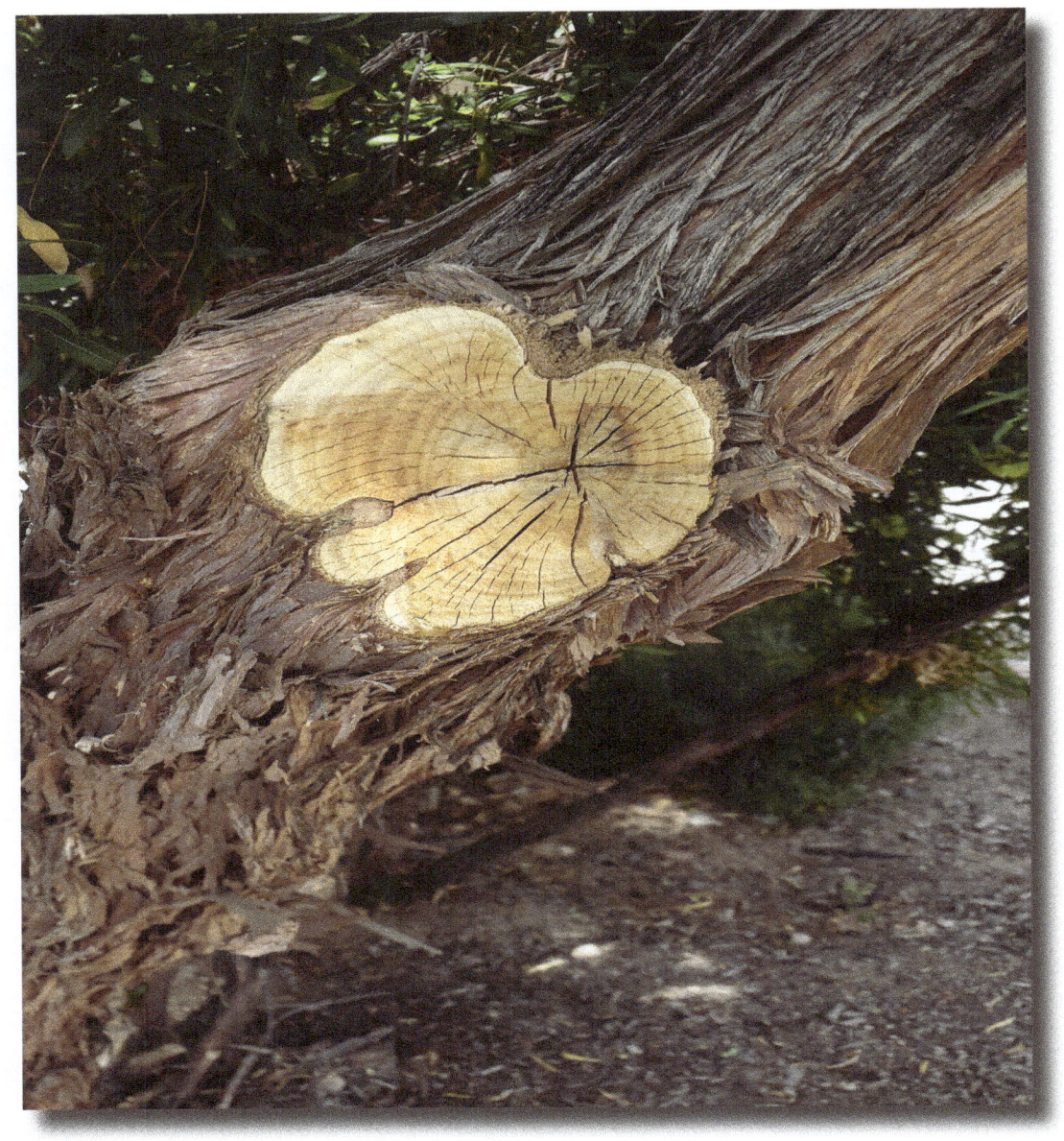

"Where there is love there is life."

~Mahatma Gandhi

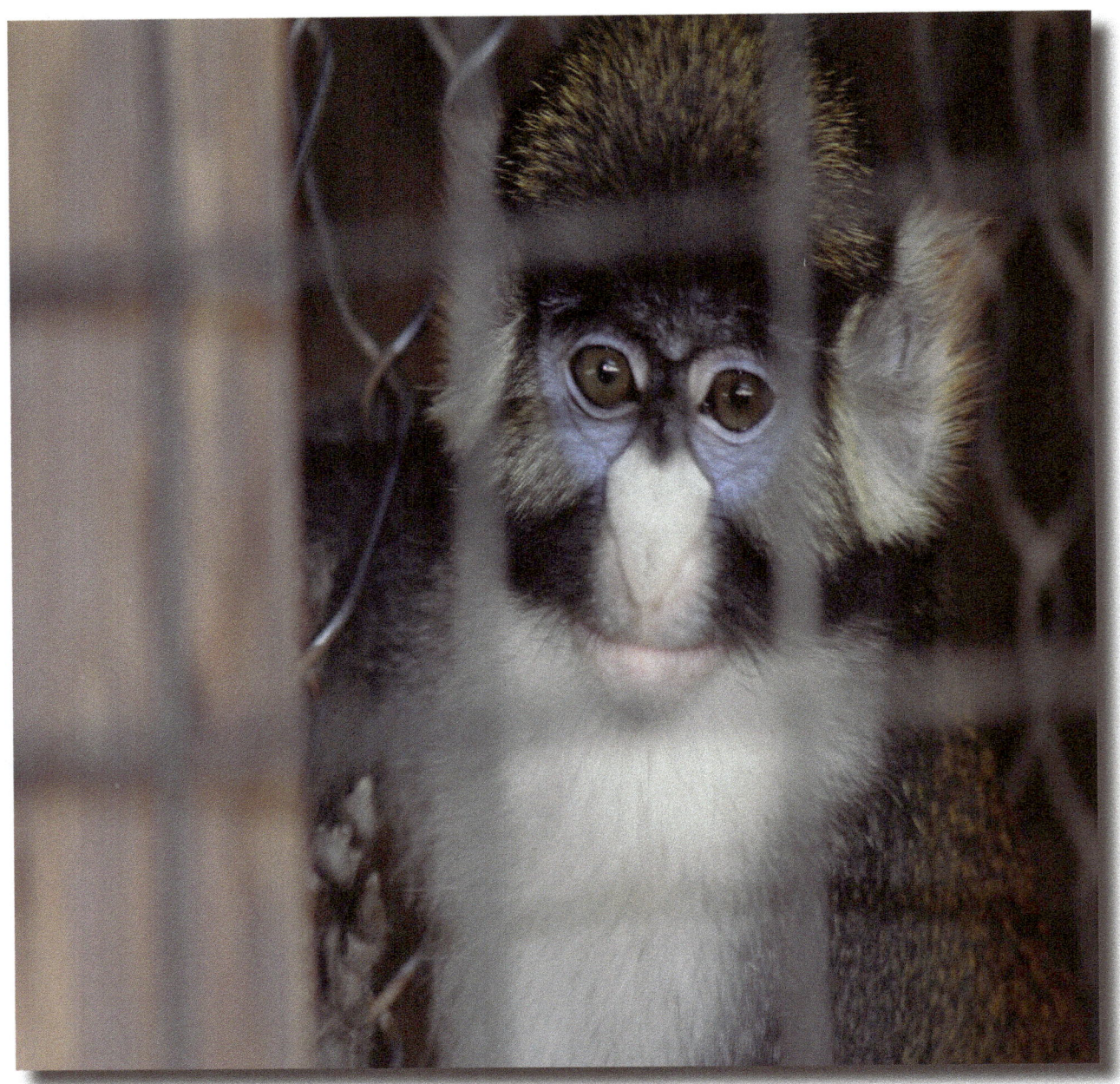

"All, everything that I understand, I only understand because I love."

~Leo Tolstoy

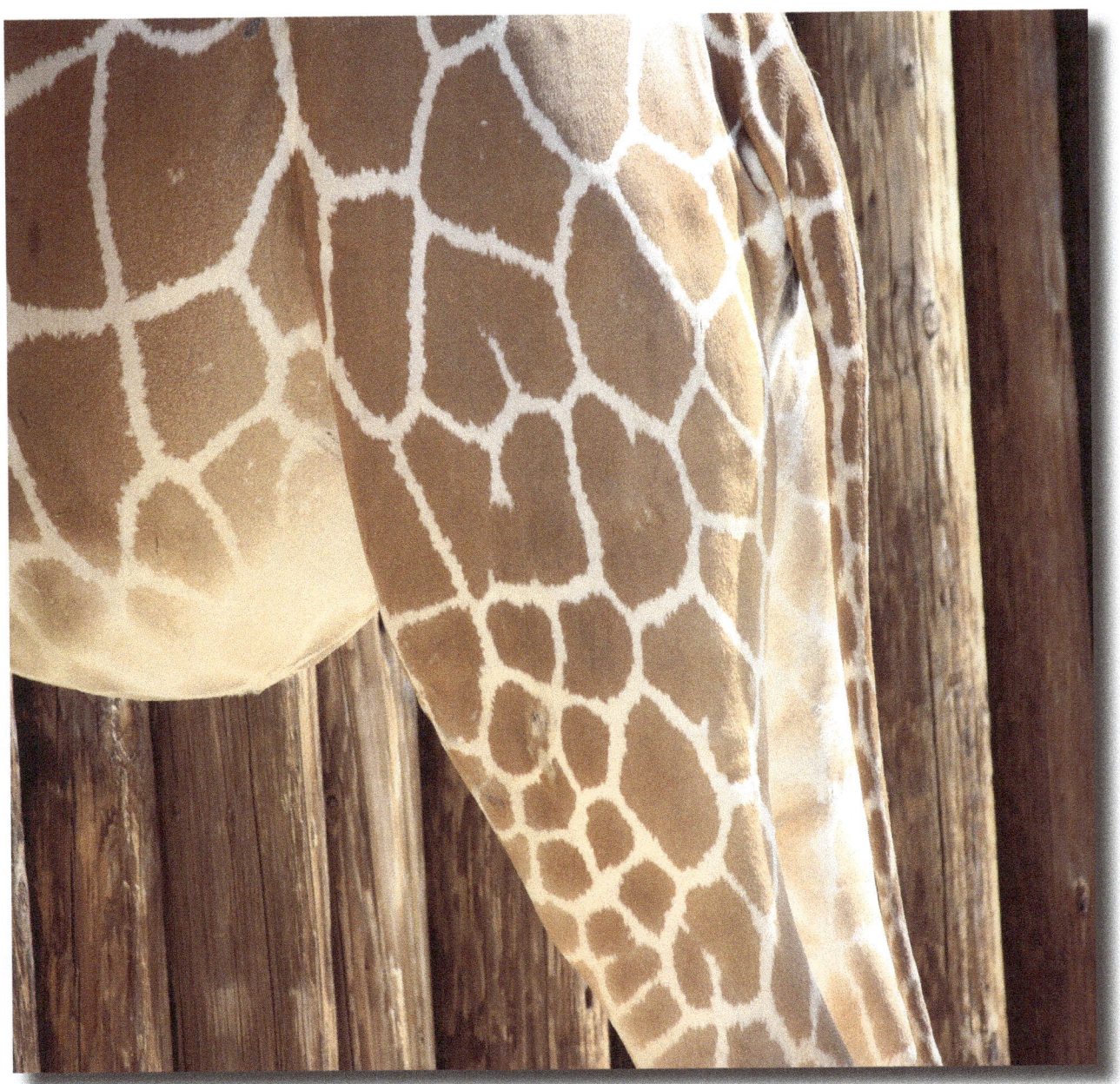

"Love is of all passions
the strongest, for it attacks
simultaneously the head, the
heart, and the senses."

~Lao Tzu

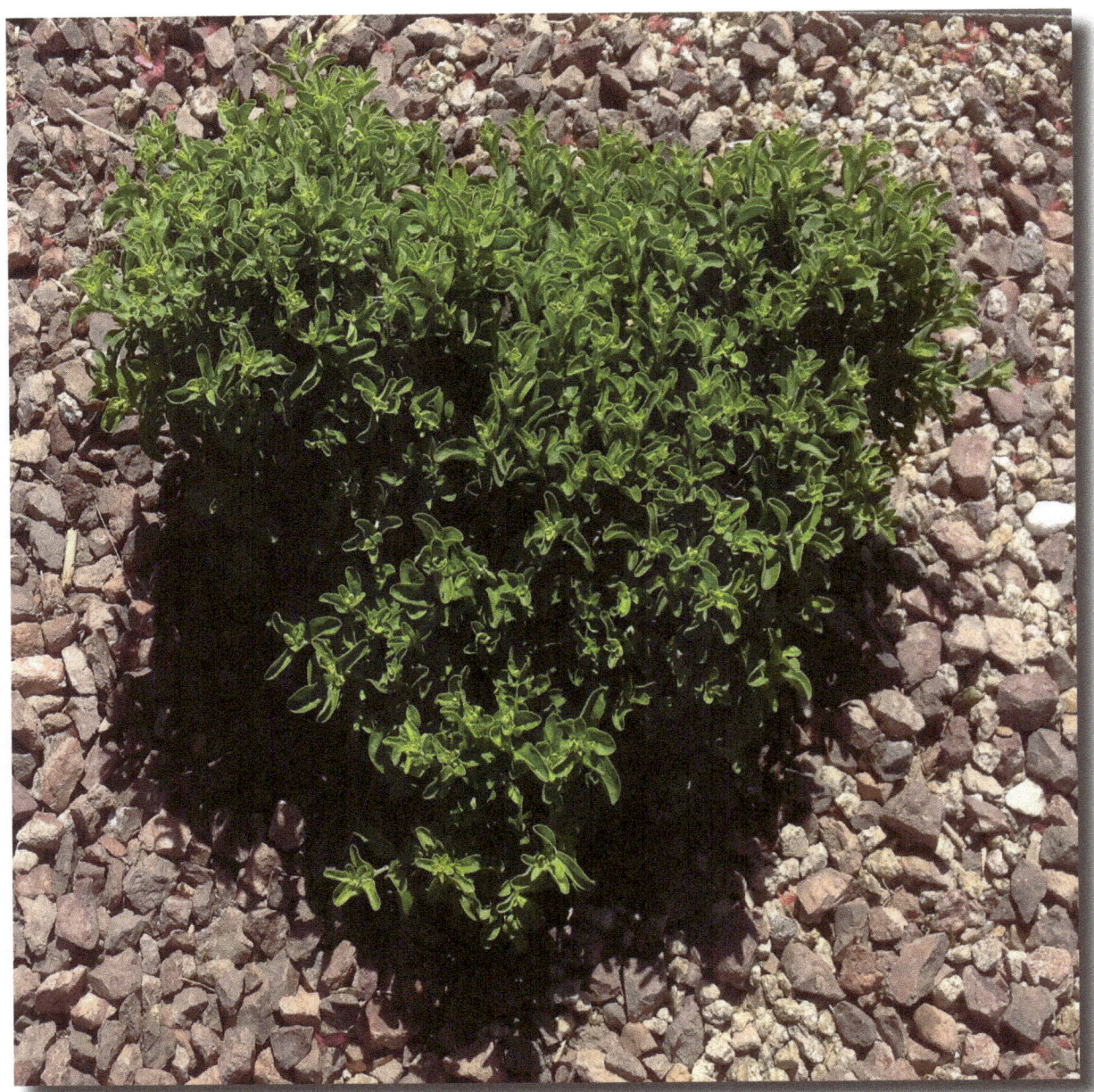

"The only thing we never get enough of is love; and the only thing we never give enough of is love".

~Henry Miller

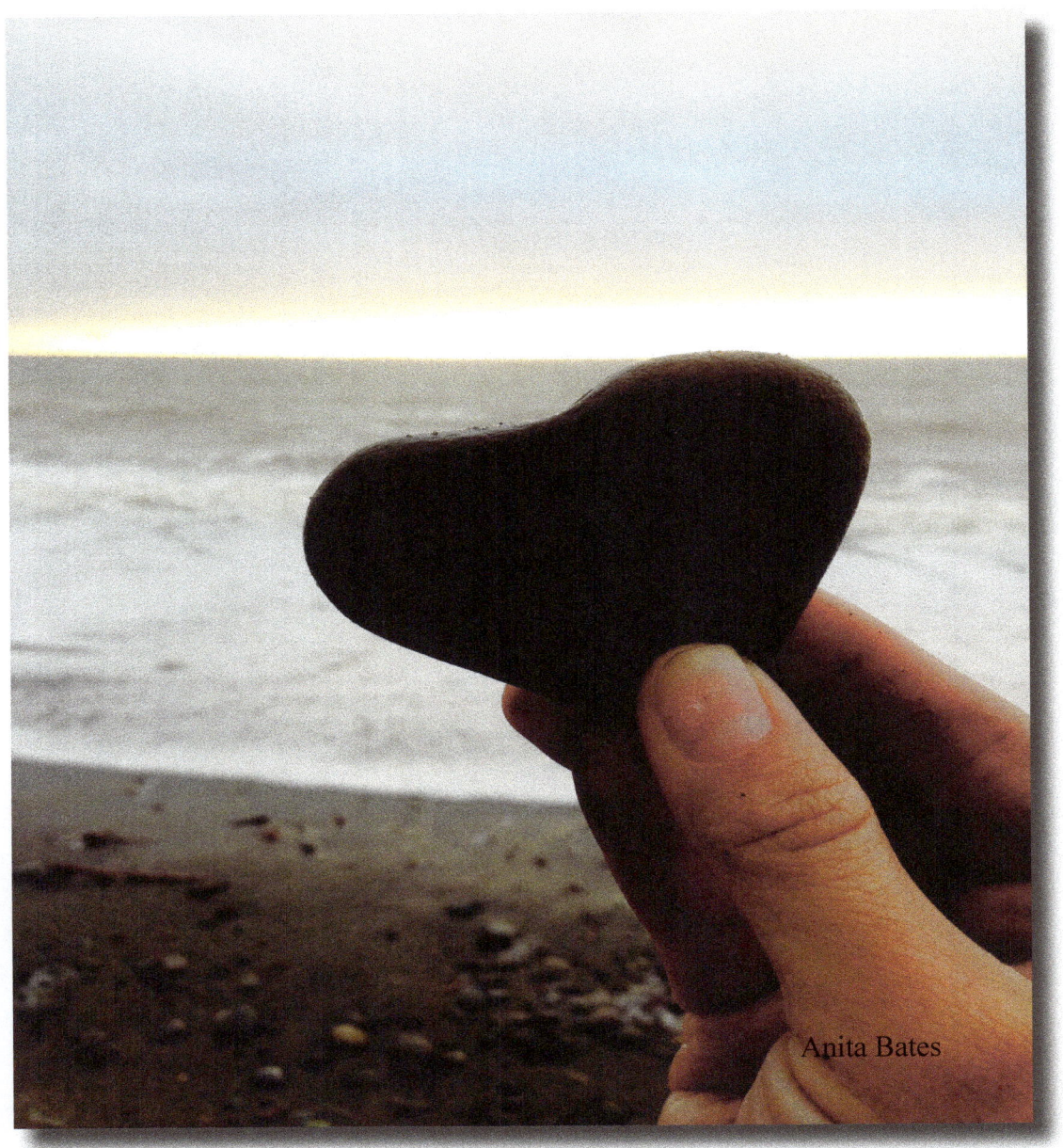

Anita Bates

" For it was not into my ear you whispered, but into my heart. It was not my lips you kissed, but my soul."

~Unknown

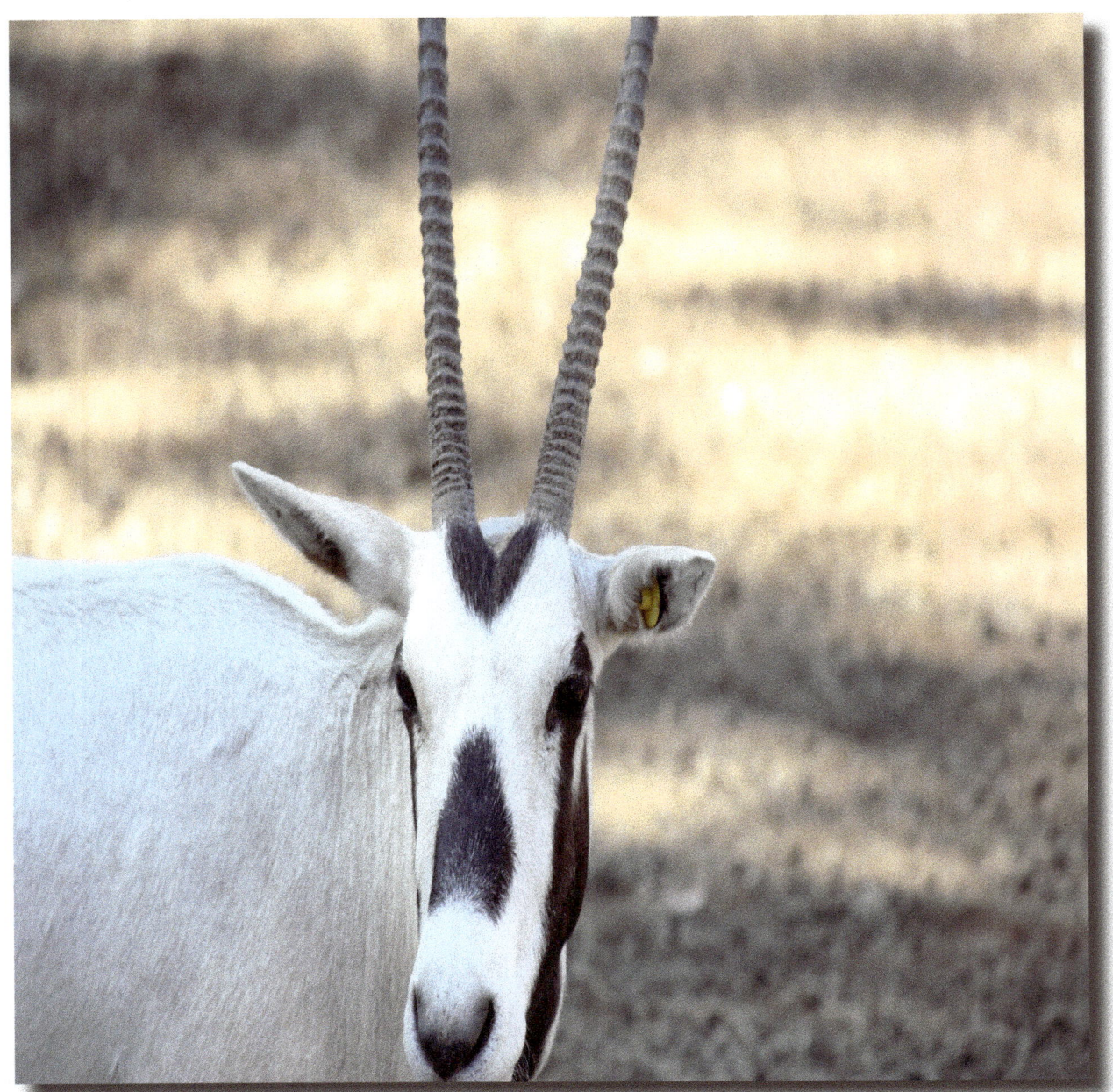

"Being deeply loved by someone gives you strength, while loving someone deeply gives you courage."

~ Lao Tzu

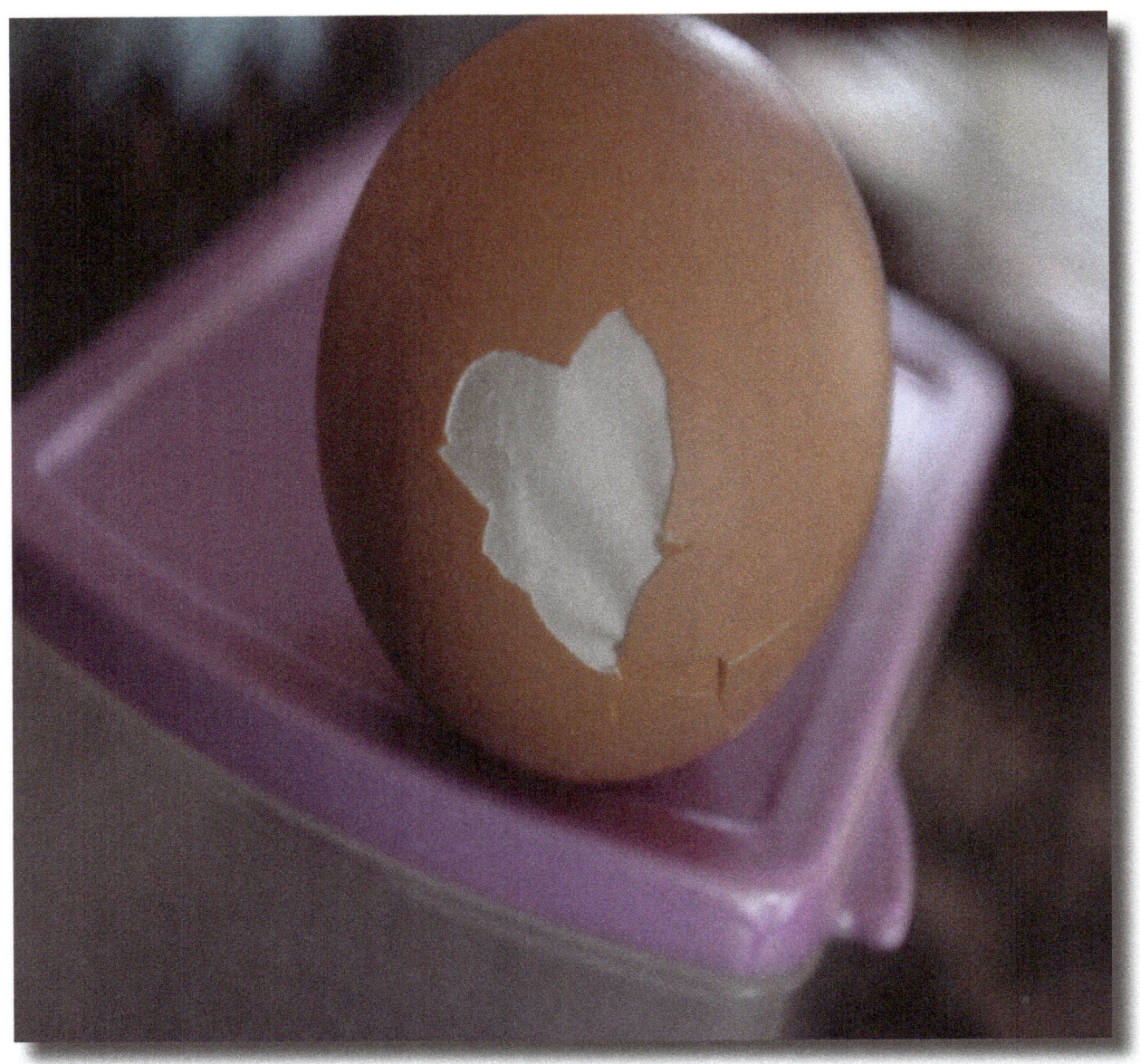

"Relationships are like glass. Sometimes it's better to leave them broken than try to hurt yourself putting it back together."

~ Unknown

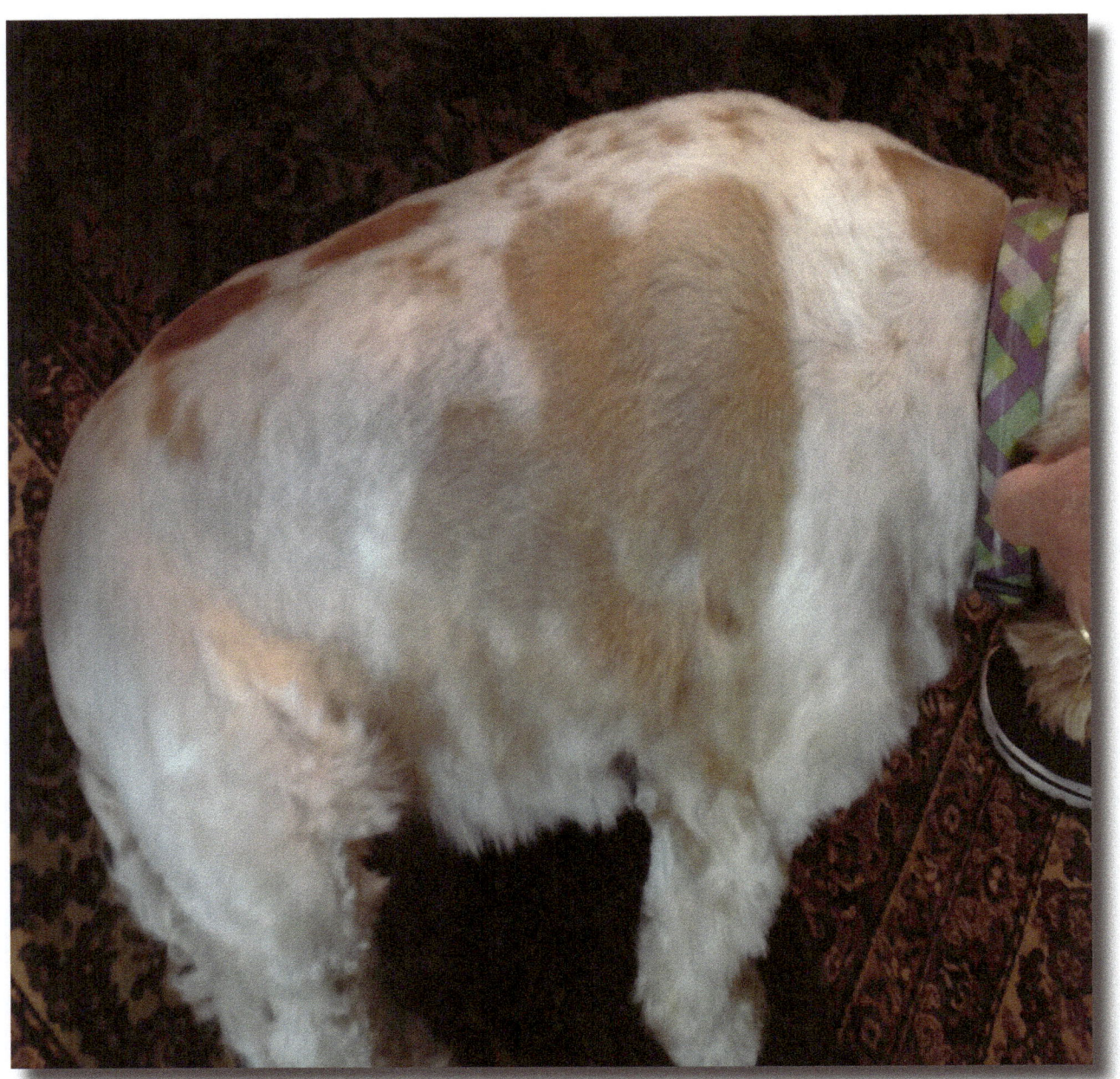

"One word frees us of all the weight and pain of life: That word is *love*."

~ Sophocles

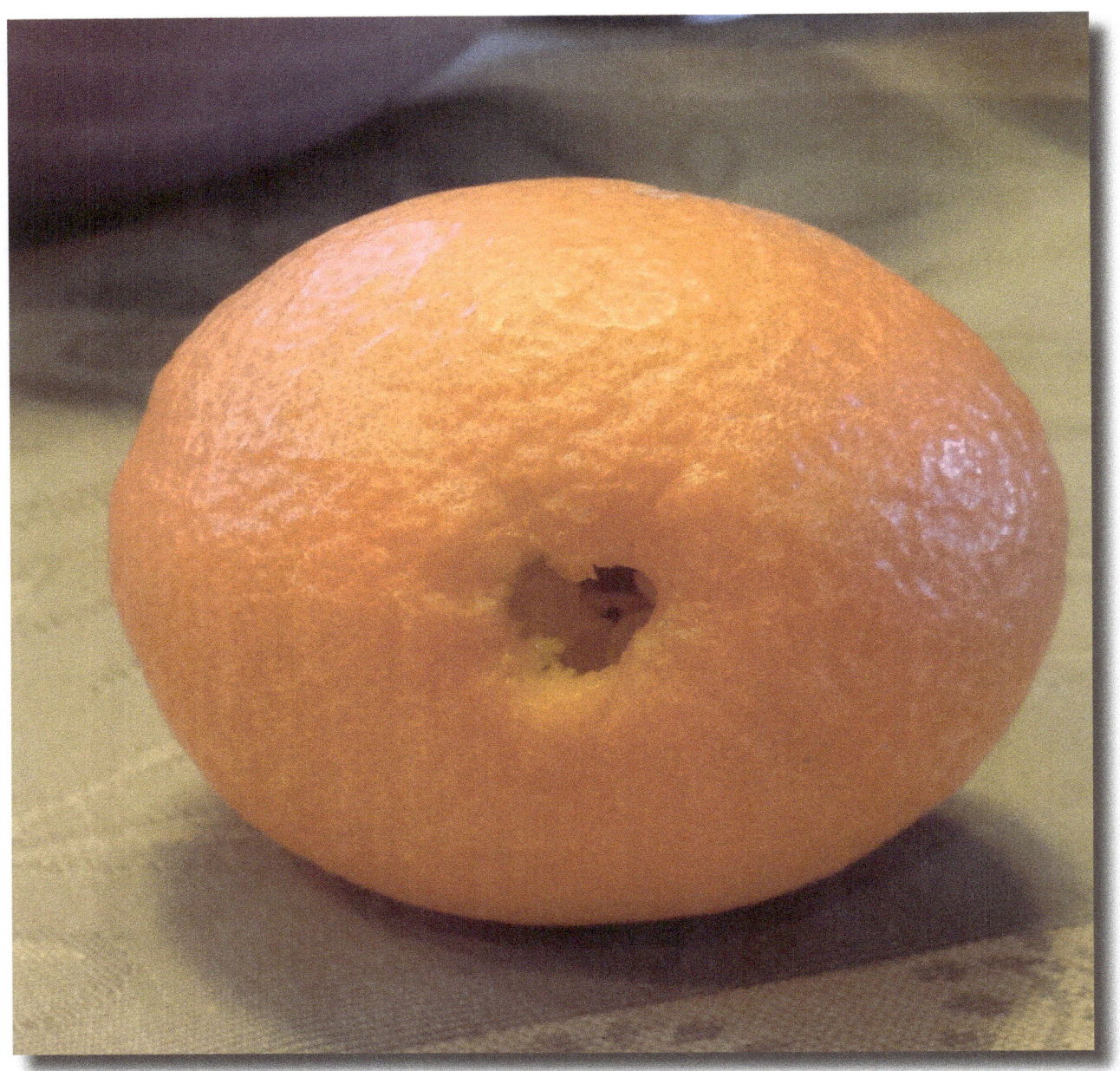

"Pleasure of love lasts but a moment. Pain of love lasts a lifetime."

~Bette Davis

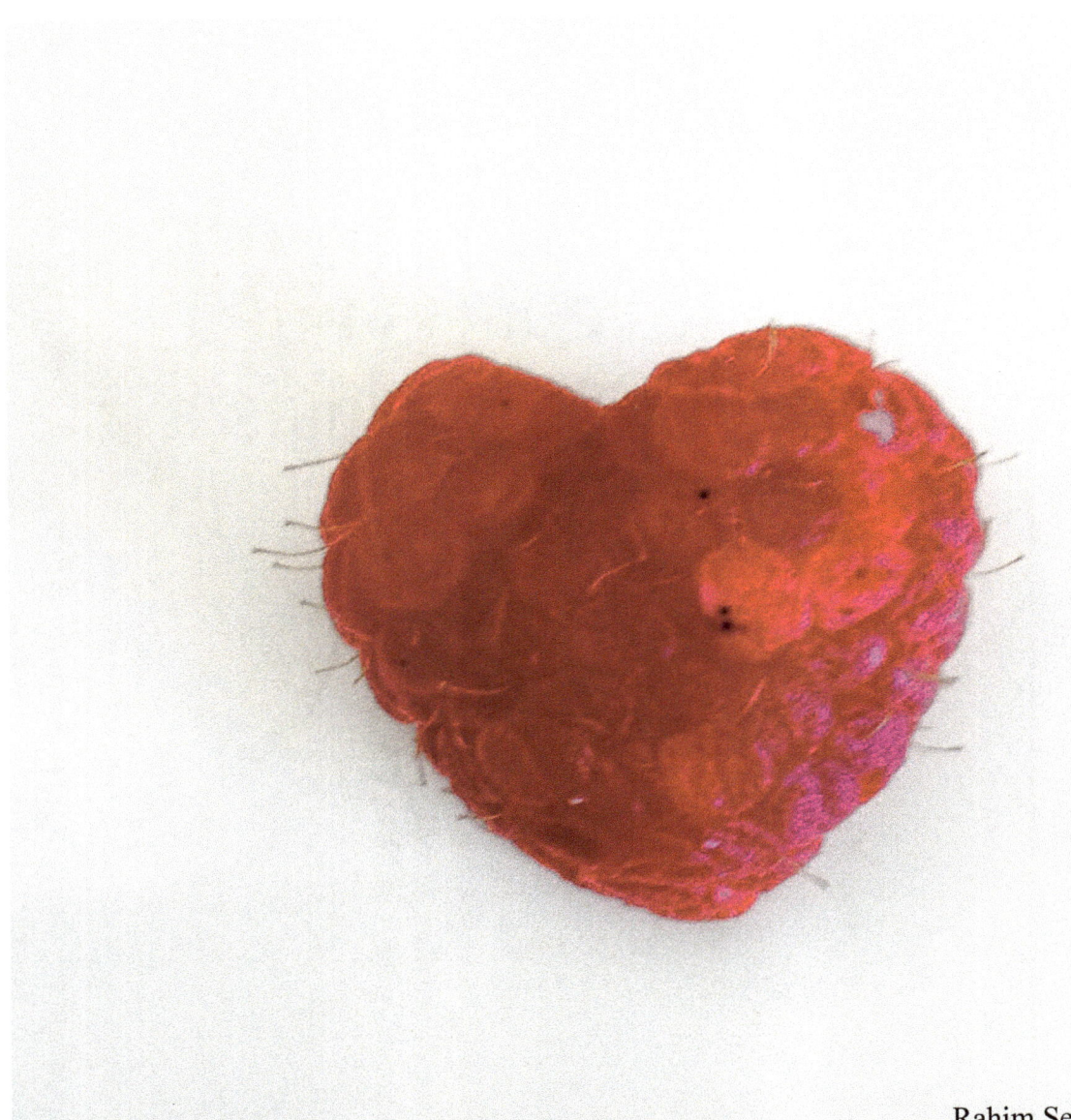

Rahim Sekandari

"Love is that condition in which the happiness of another person is essential to your own."

~ Robert A. Heinlein

"You've got to dance like there's nobody watching. Love like you'll never be hurt. Sing like there's nobody listening. And live like it's heaven on earth".

~William W. Purkey

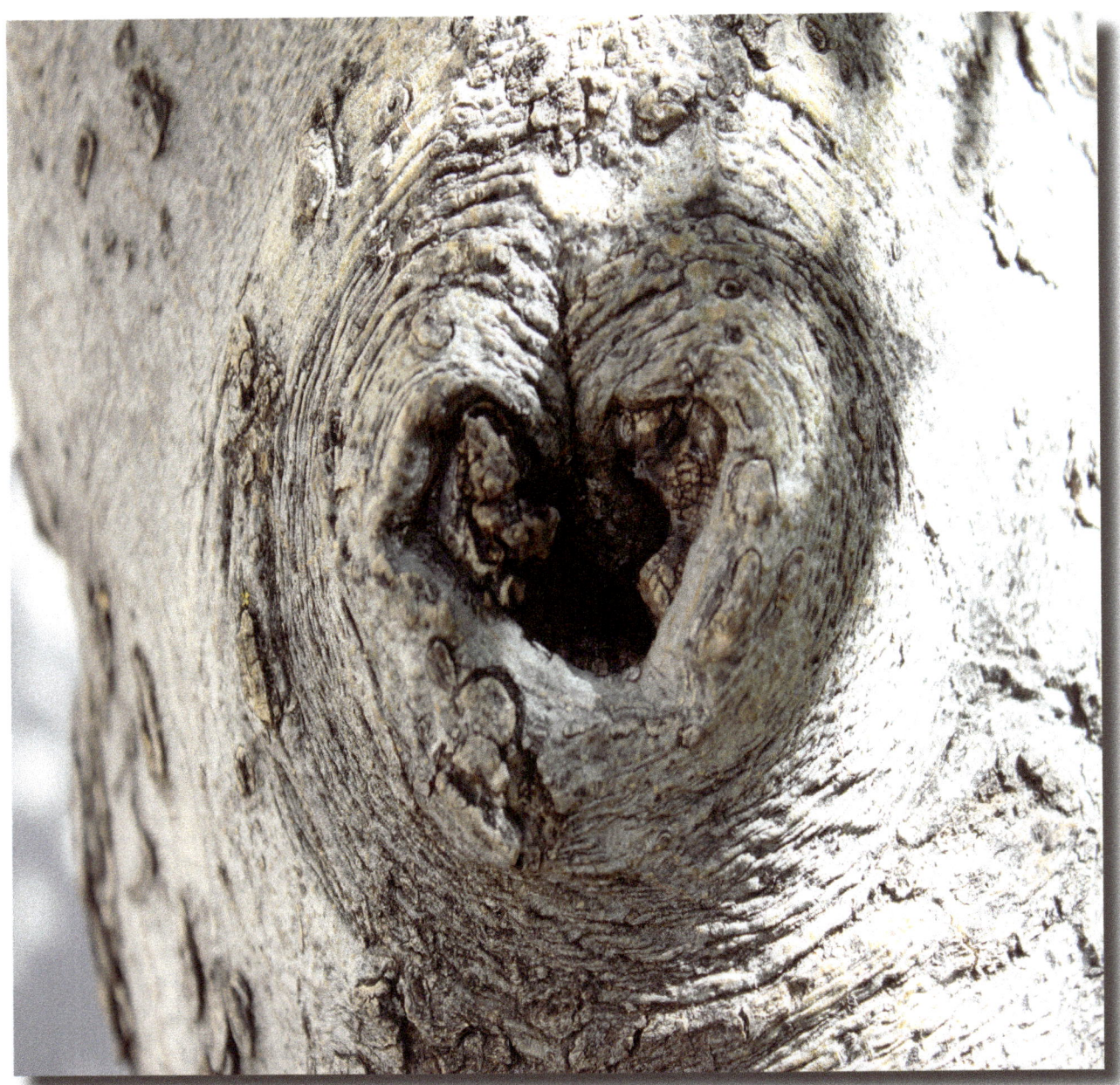

"We don't love qualities, we love a person; sometimes by reason of their defects as well as their qualities."

~ Jacques Maritain

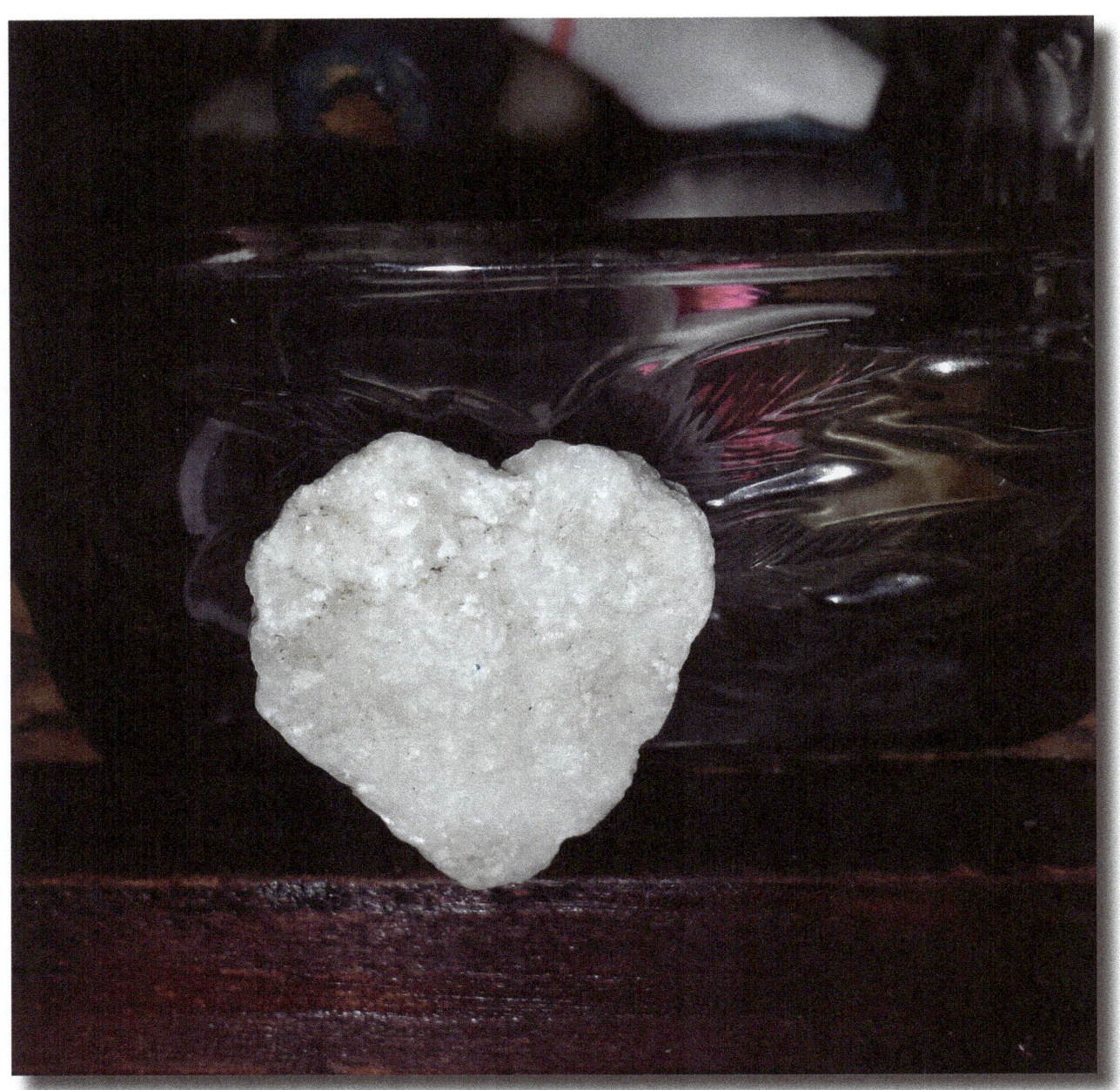

"A loving heart is the truest wisdom"

~ Charles Dickens

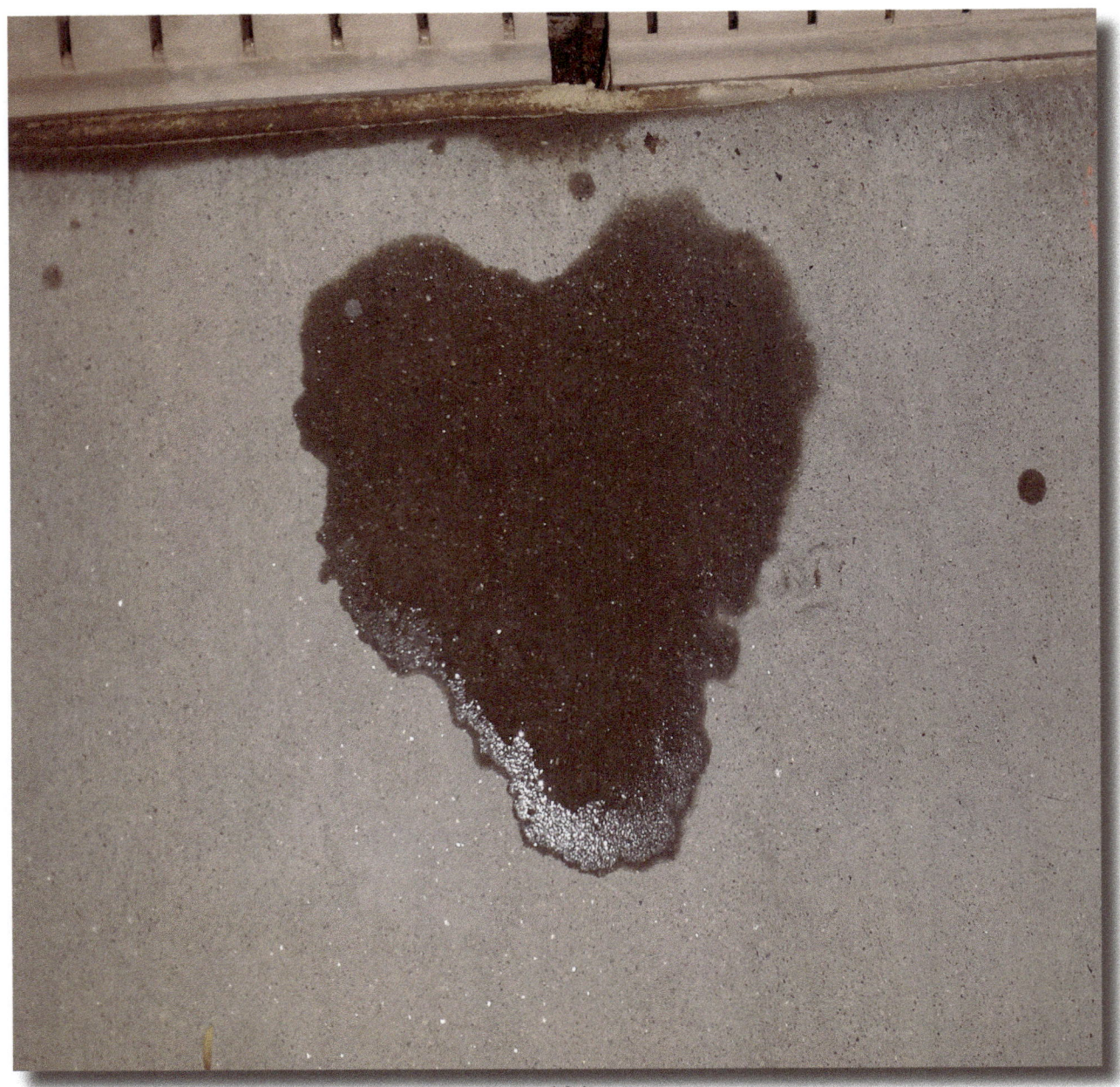

"To love is to place our happiness in the happiness of another"

~ G.W. Leibniz

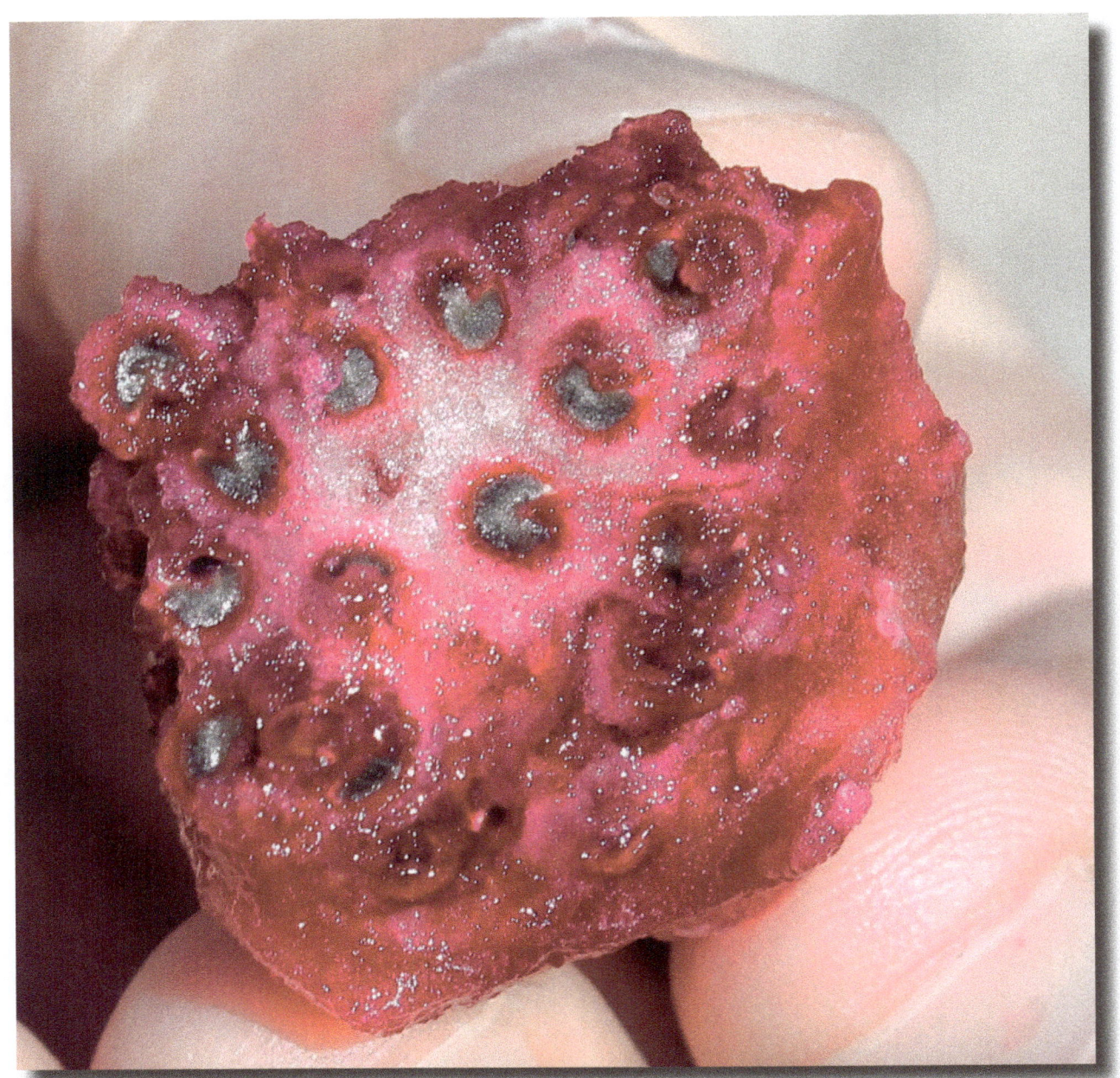

"Two people in love, alone, isolated from the world, that's beautiful."

~Milan Kundera

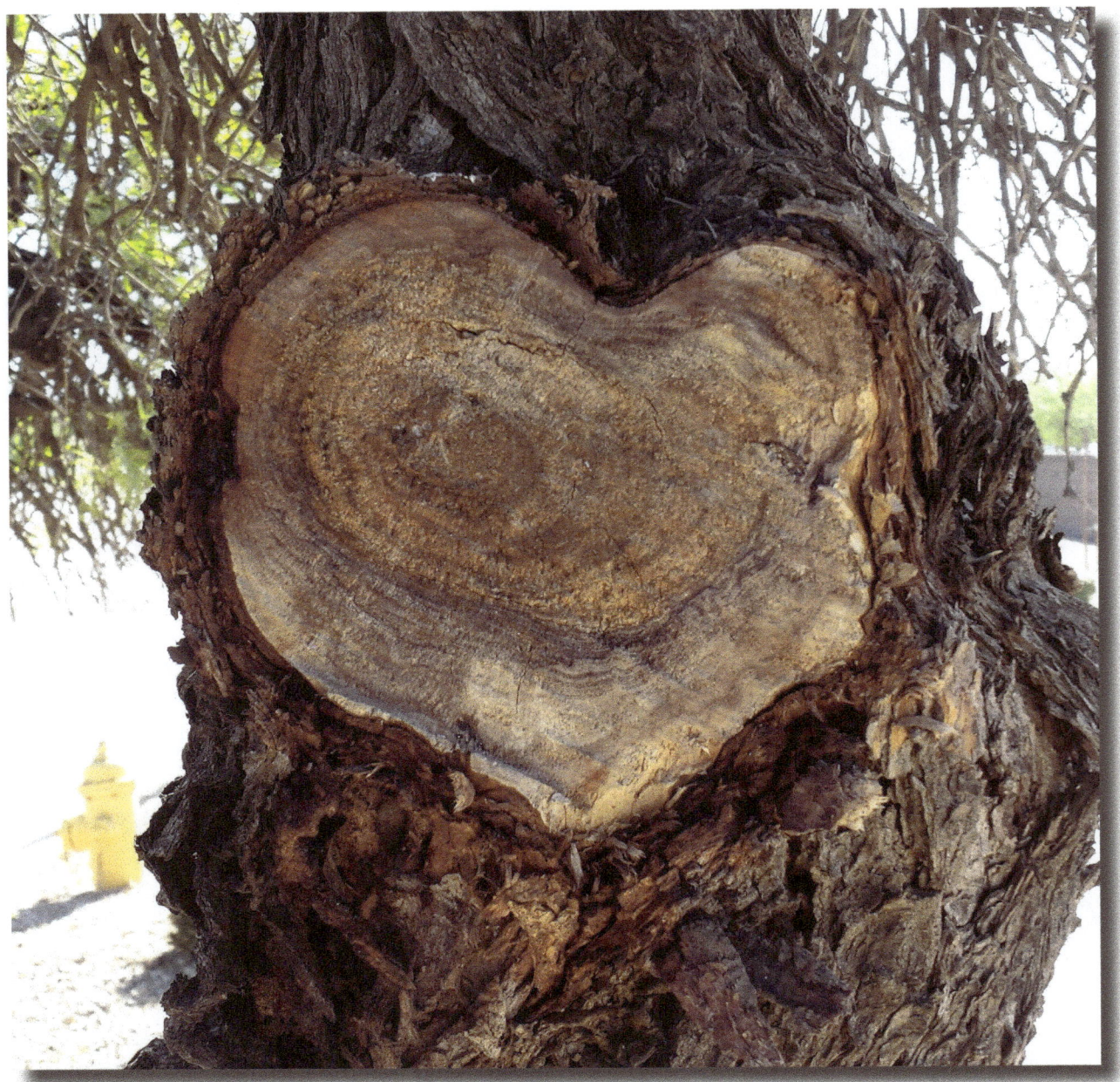

"I have found the paradox, that if you love until it hurts, there can be no more hurt, only more love."

~Mother Teresa

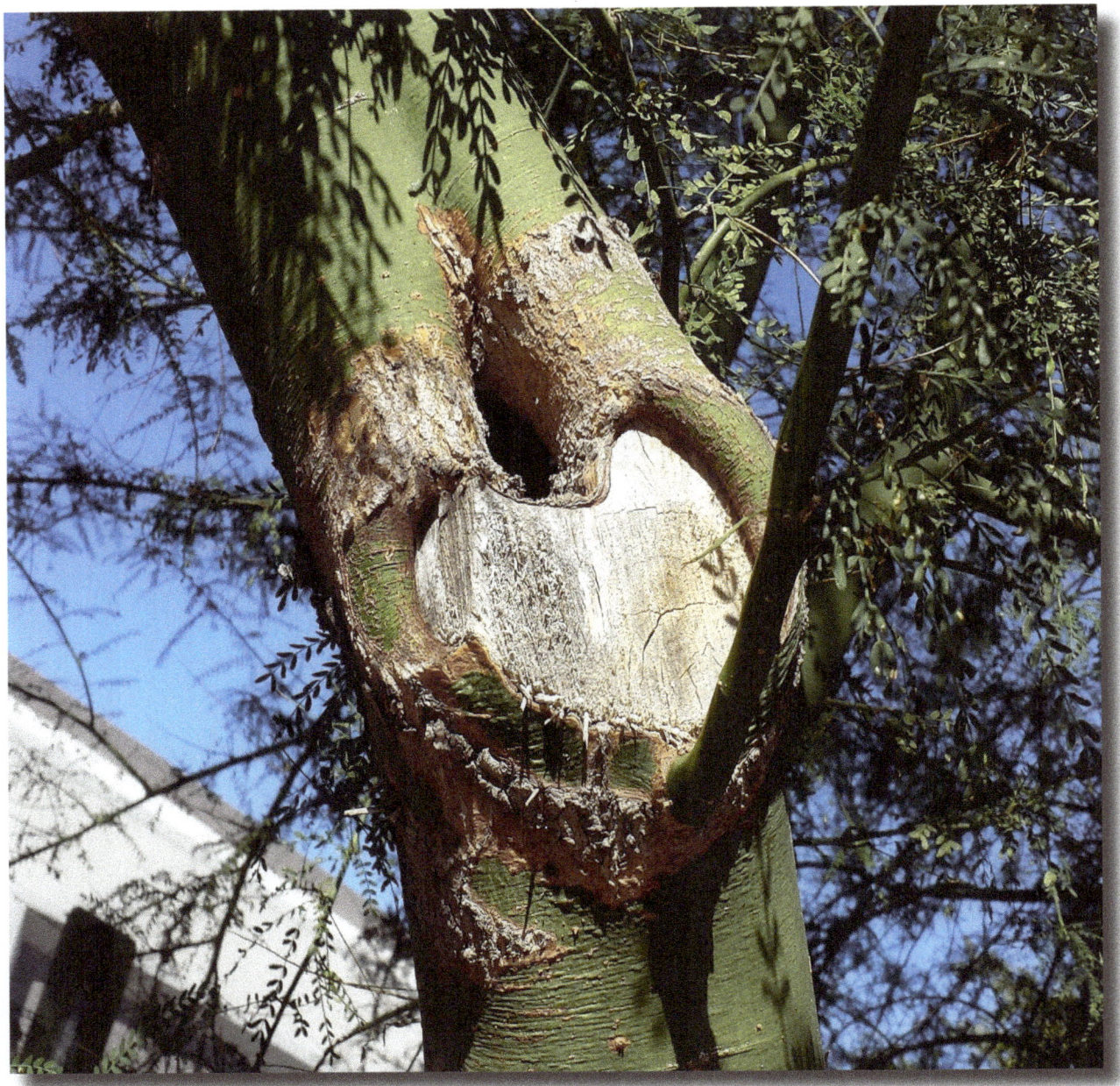

"The heart that loves is always young."

~Greek Proverb

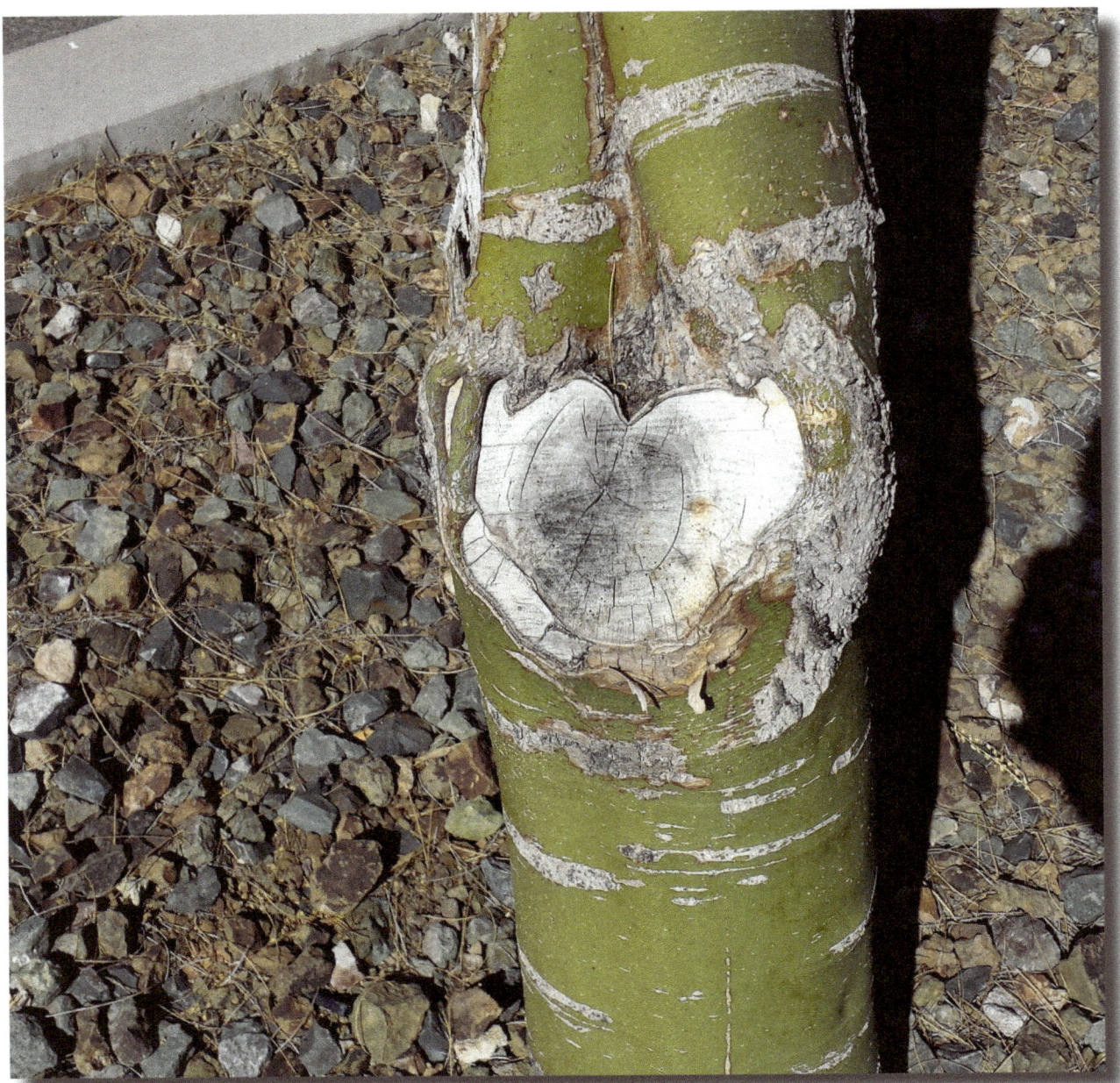

"Gravitation is not responsible for people falling in love."

~Albert Einstein

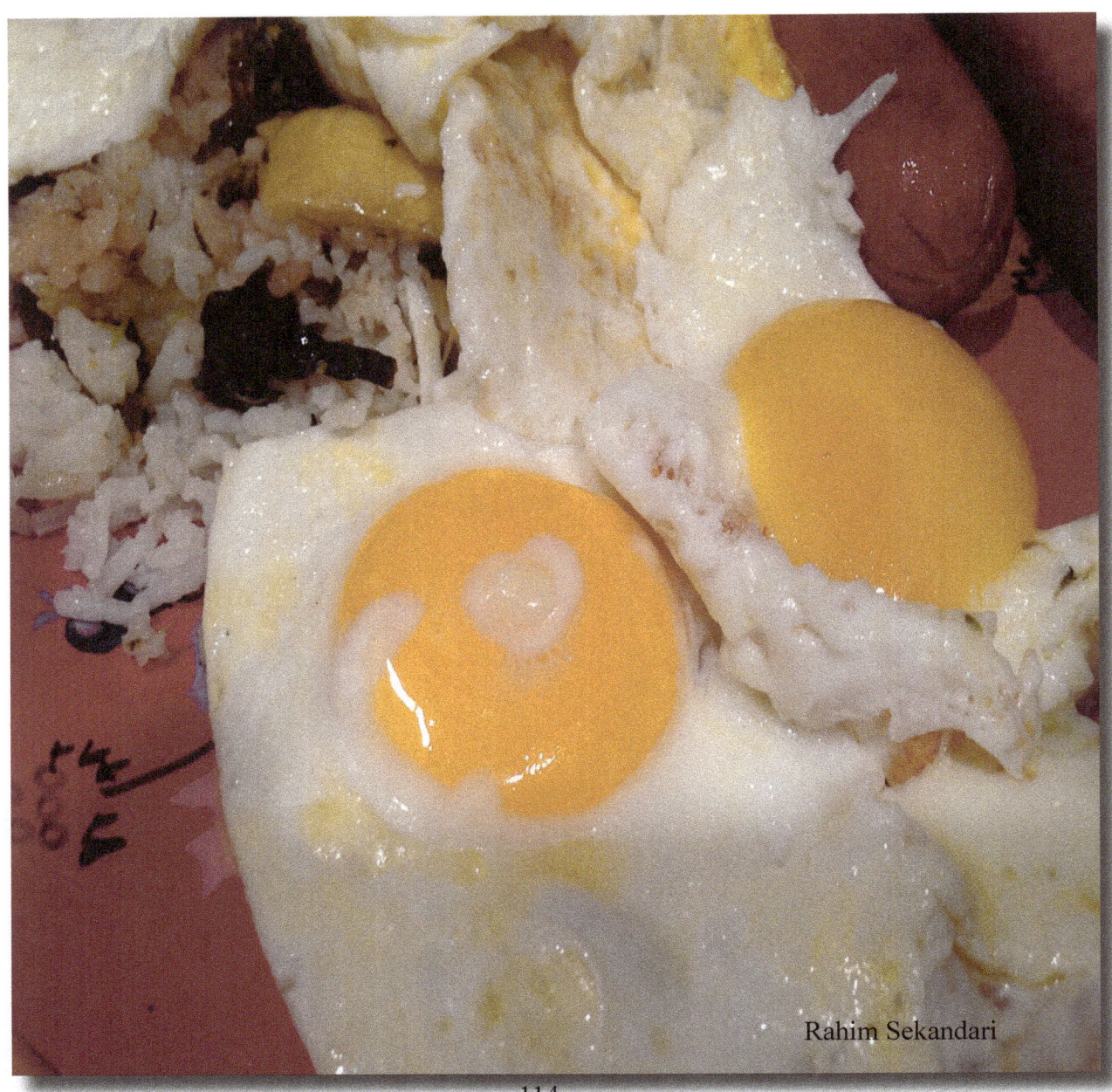

Rahim Sekandari

"Have a heart that never hardens, a temper that never tires, and a touch that never hurts."

~Charles Dickens

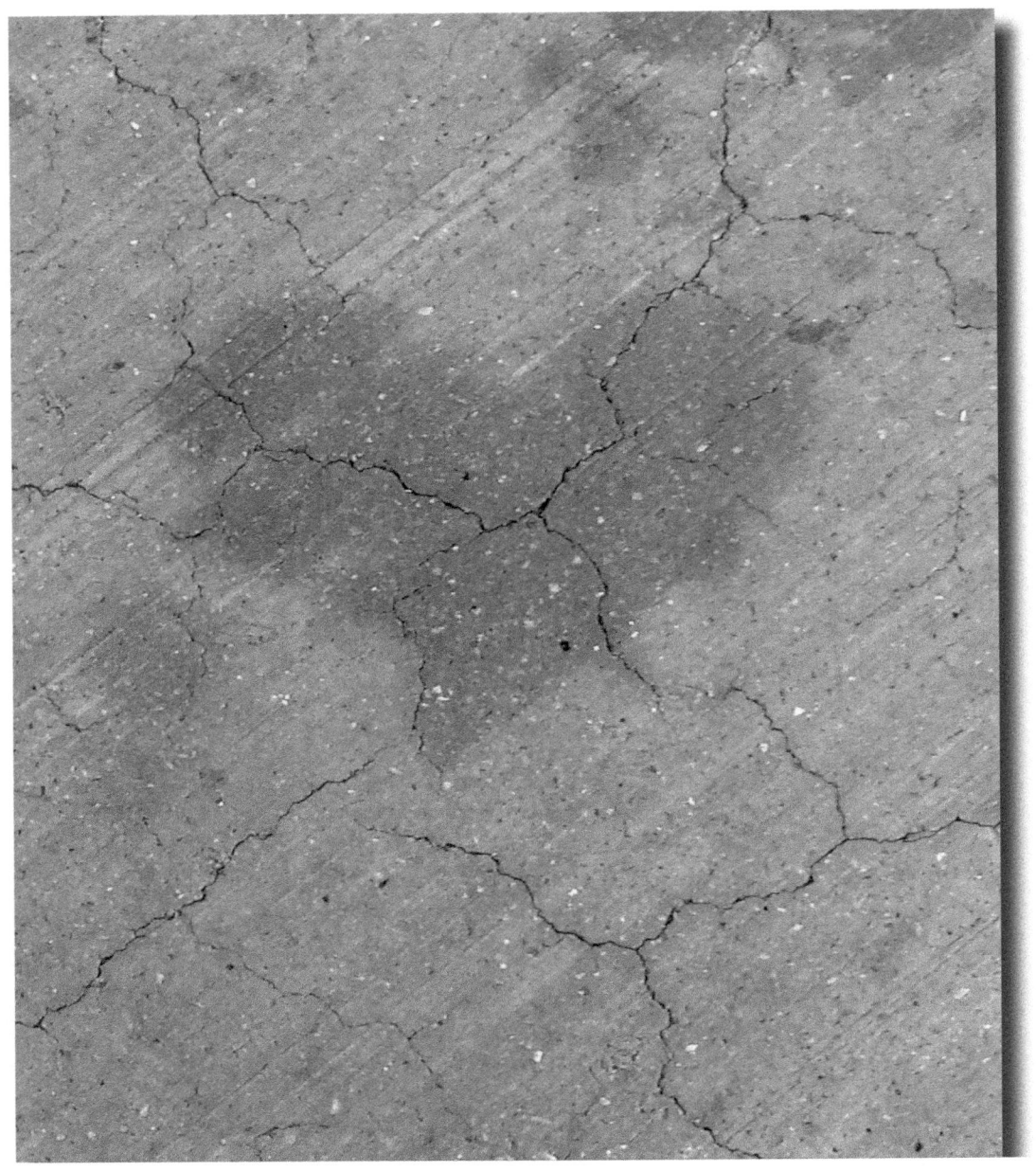

"Keep love in your heart. A life without it is like a sunless garden when the flowers are dead."

~Oscar Wilde

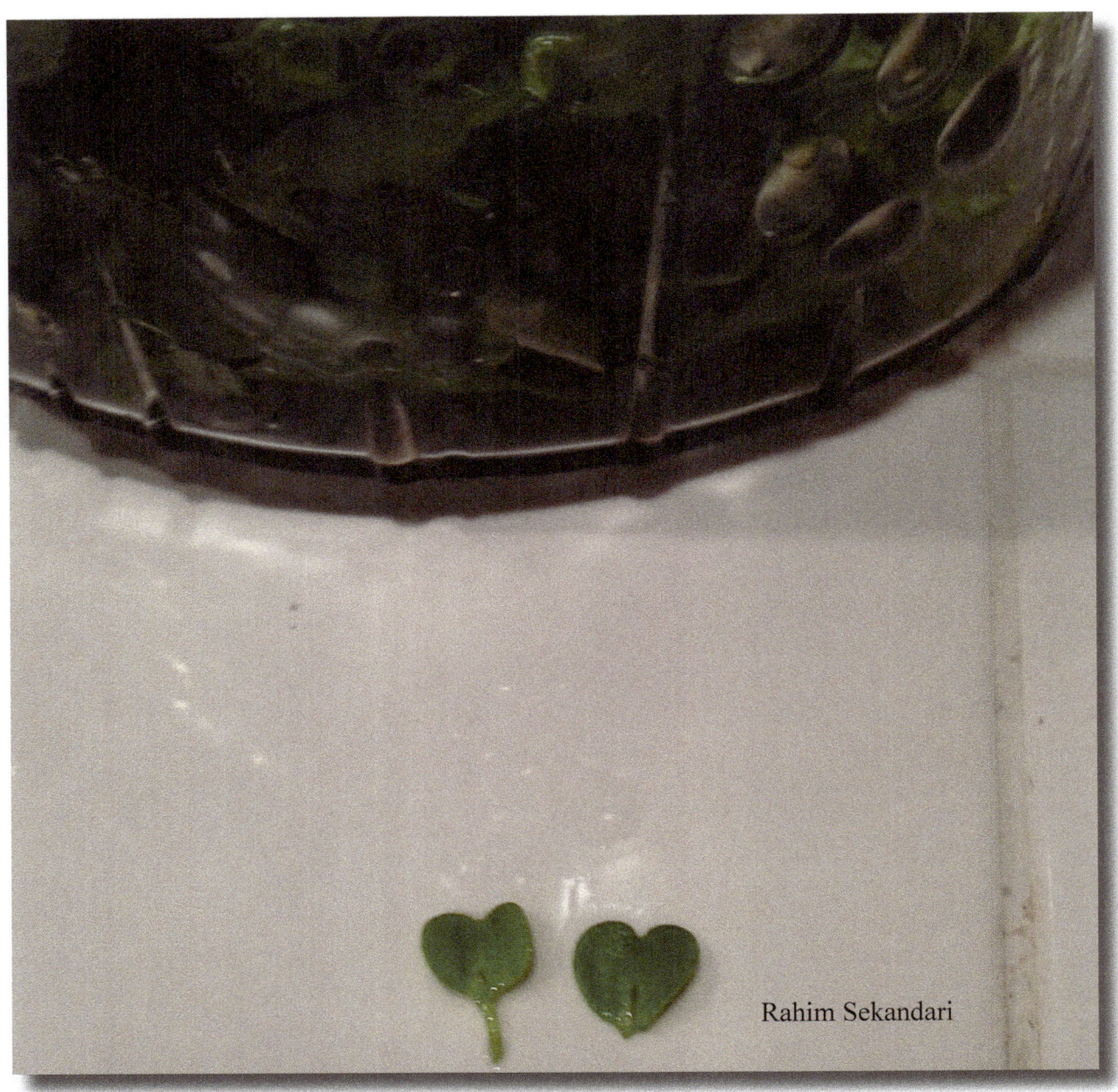

Rahim Sekandari

"It is better in prayer to have a heart without words than words without a heart"

~ Mahatma Gandhi

The Back Story

The pictures found in this book were gathered by the authors along with various friends and family. Each picture tells it's own story but some have an interesting back story as well.

Page 2: The author's uncle, Rahim Sekandari, took this picture on one of his regular morning hikes in Tucson, AZ.

Page 4: The water puddle heart was found during a morning walk to school by the authors.

Page 6: The heart shaped leaf was found on the grass at the authors house.

Page 8: The heart shaped bite of Khajour (an Afghan dessert) was made by the authors.

Page 10: The cactus heart was taken by Rahim Sekandari during a morning hike in Tucson, AZ.

Page 12: The street heart shaped pot hole in the street was discovered during a routine morning walk to school by the authors.

Page 14: The perfect heart rock was found in the snow by Rahim Sekandari.

Page 16: The heart water stain was left at Rahim Sekandari's house after he watered the plants.

Page 18: The heart shaped snow was observed by the authors while on vacation at Big Bear Lake, CA

Page 20: The perfect heart was noticed by the authors during a conference presentation in AZ

Page 22: The heart shape cut in the tree was found at Gilroy Gardens, in San Jose, CA.

Page 24: The heart water puddle was discovered by Rahim Sekandari while walking in his new neighborhood in Germany.

Page 26: The heart grease mark was found by authors on morning walk to school.

Page 28: The heart shaped raisin in the Ezekiel raisin and cinnamon bread was found by the authors.

Page 30: The heart shaped sea weed was found on the beach in San Diego, CA.

Page 32: The heart shaped spoon mark in hummus was noticed by the authors after making the hummus.

Page 34: The heart stain by the road crack was noticed by the authors during their usual morning walk to school.

Page 36: The heart shaped dried bananas was found by the authors.

Page 38: While visiting family, the elusive heart cloud was spotted at last by the authors during a morning hike in Lakeside, AZ,

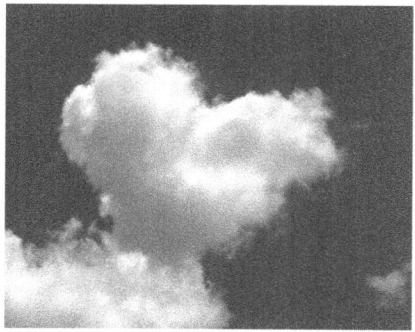

Page 40: The heart shaped peanut brittle was noticed by the authors.

Page 42: The heart shaped pickles were served to Rahim Sekandari, while dining at a restaurant.

Page 44: The heart shaped cactus was spotted by Rahim Sekandari, during morning hike in Tucson, AZ.

Page 46: The heart shaped strawberry was served to Rahim Sekandari while dining in a restaurant in Germany.

Page 48: The heart shaped pot hole was found on a walk through the neighborhood by the authors.

Page 50: The heart shaped stain on the saucer was discovered after breakfast in San Jose by the authors.

Page 52: The heart shaped sea weed was found on the beach by the authors in San Diego ,CA

Page 54: The heart on the food container was the result of left over yogurt from lunch by the authors.

Page 56: The heart shaped water puddle and pot hole were discovered on a walk through the neighborhood by the authors.

Page 58: The heart shaped radish was found by Rahim Sekandari, as he was making salad.

Page 60: The heart in the road was found by the authors while driving through Navajo Nation in northern Arizona.

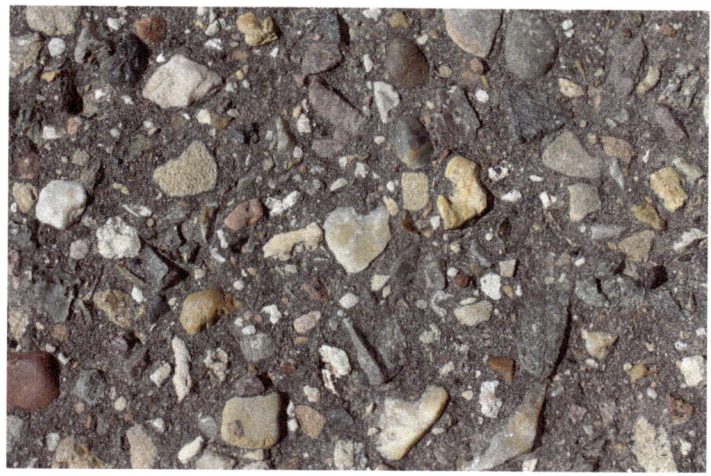

Page 62: The heart toast was provided by Mujghan Mojaddidi.

Page 64: The heart rock was discovered in Payson, AZ by Ilyas Sekandari

Page 66: The heart shaped cream on the plate was taken by Hasina Mojaddidi while eating dinner at a restaurant. The potatoes on her plate left the heart shape.

Page 68: The heart swans were the result of perfect timing of two paddle boats coming together at Gilroy Gardens in San Jose, CA.

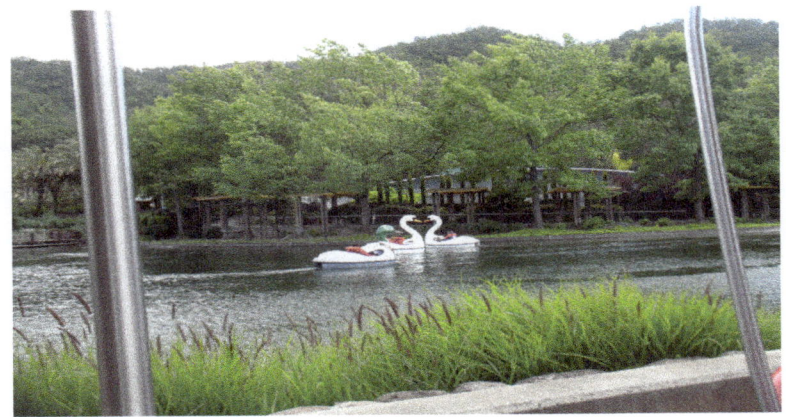

Page 70: The heart rock was discovered by Aleah Sekandari at Payson, AZ.

Page 72: The heart stain on the road was discovered by the authors while walking in the neighborhood.

Page 74: The paw with the heart shaped foot pad was from a leopard at the Wild Life Zoo, in Litchfield AZ. The leopard was taking a nap on a cage above where the authors were standing.

Page 76: The heart shape in the nose of the bobcat skull was seen during a nature presentation in Phoenix, AZ

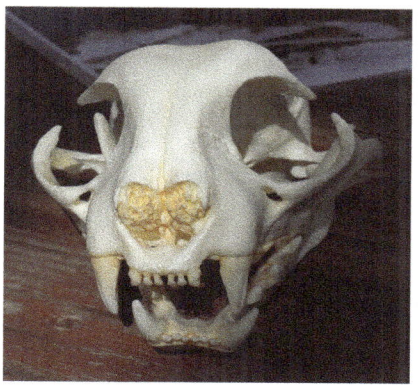

Page 78: The heart shaped cut of the tree limb was found at a friends house by the authors during a visit.

Page 80: The Schmidt's spotnose Guenon African Monkey with it's heart shaped nose at the Wild Life Zoo in Litchfield, AZ

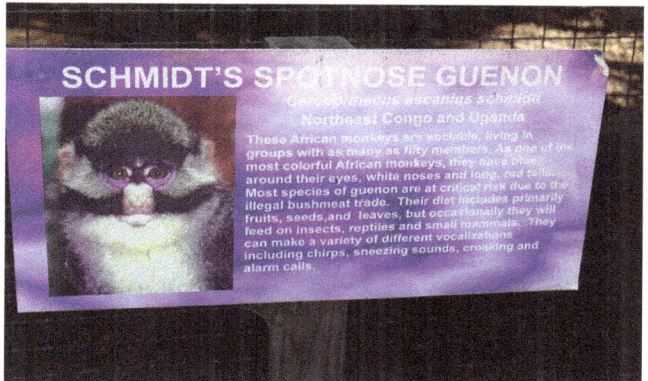

Page 82: The giraffe with heart shapes on it's leg was at the Wild Life zoo in Litchfield, AZ

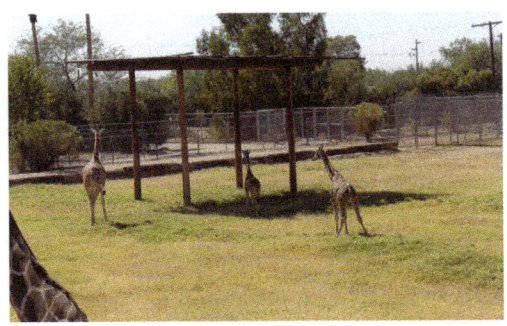

Page 84: The heart shaped bush was just growing out when the picture was taken. Several months later, the bush no longer resembled a heart.

 Page 86: A long time friend of the author's found this picture on her Facebook page and asked her friend if we could use the picture. The picture was taken by Anita Bates at the Dungeness National Wildlife Refuge in Washington State. She found the rock while walking on the beach.

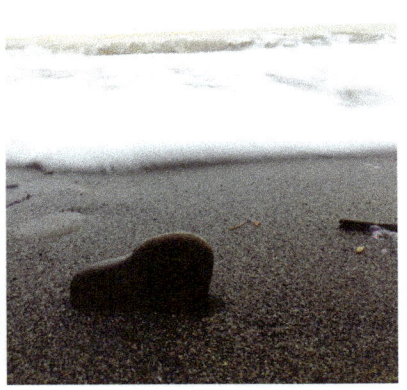

Page 88: The gazelle with the heart shape on the forehead was spotted at the Wild Life zoo at Litchfield, AZ during a field trip by the authors.

Page 90: As the egg was being peeled by the authors, a heart shape emerged.

Page 92: Molly is the most wonderful and loving dog. She really does wear her heart on her coat. The picture was taken by authors.

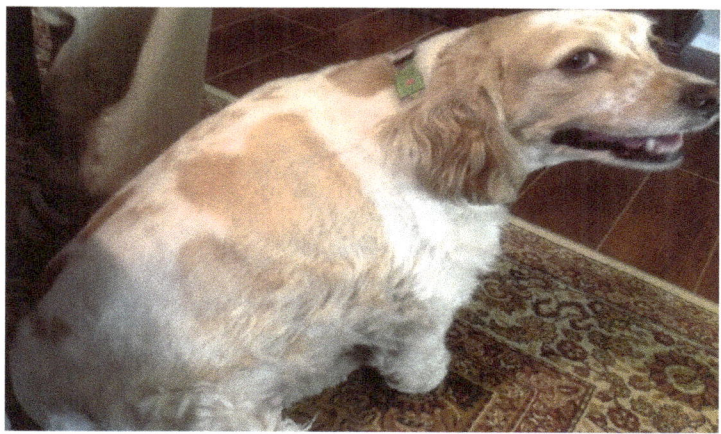

Page 94: Sarah Jurak was peeling an orange during a family gathering and noticed the heart after removing the stem.

Page 96: Rahim Sekandari submitted the heart shaped raspberry picture.

Page 98: The heart shaped blackberry was in a fresh package of blackberries found by the authors.

Page 100: The beautiful heart knot in the tree was found by the authors during a hot summer day hike at Saguaro Lake, AZ.

Page 102: The heart rock was found on moving day by the authors in their back yard.

Page 104: The heart water stain was noticed in the back yard during a pool party by the authors. The water by the pool was drying up into the perfect heart shape after everyone left the pool.

Page 106: The authors discovered prickly pears for the first time while visiting Tucson, AZ. To their amazement, when they cut the pear in half, the center revealed heart shaped seeds.

Page 108: The authors discovered this heart on a walk while waiting for car service.

Page 110: The heart was discovered on a walk by the authors.

Page 112: The heart was seen by the authors during a walk in the neighborhood.

Page 114: Rahim Sekandari noticed the heart in his eggs while cooking breakfast.

Page 116: The authors noticed the heart stain while getting gas at Costco.

Page 118: Rahim Sekandari found the heart micro greens while making salad.

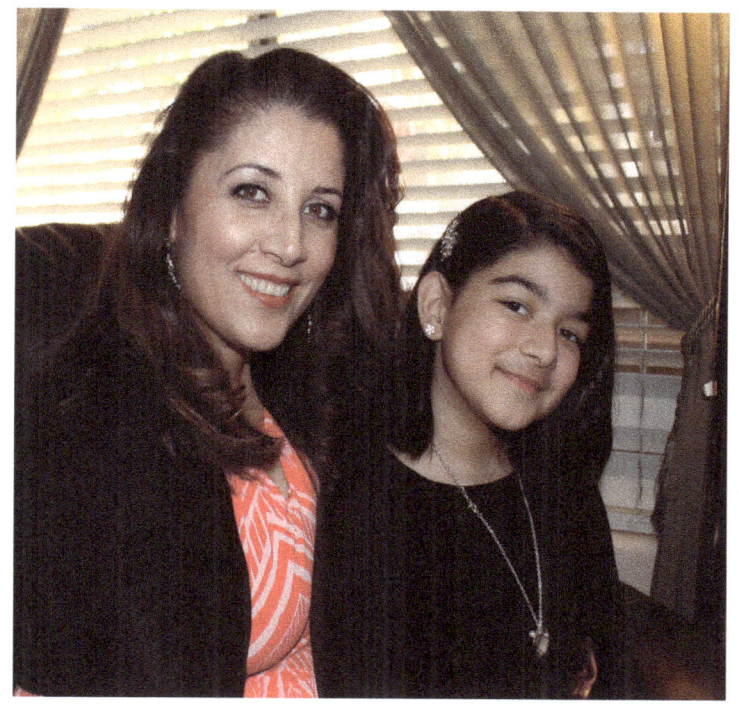

Nafisa Sekandari is the proud mother of Malia and full time psychologist in private practice. Nafisa Sekandari is also the author of the popular book "Afghan Cuisine Cookbook: A Collection of Family Recipes" available on amazon.com.

Malia Sekandari, currently in the 4th grade, came up with the concept of this book when she was just 4 years old. She is a bright, funny, creative and highly imaginative 9 year old. This is the first of many books to be written and published by Malia.

Love is hidden in small Places

www.ingramcontent.com/pod-product-compliance
Lightning Source LLC
Chambersburg PA
CBHW041345210526
45162CB00016B/10